WHAT SHIP IS THAT?

WHAT SHIP IS THAT?

Written and Illustrated by
Bobby L. Basnight

THE LYONS PRESS

To MARY LYALL *and* LANE

Printed in the United States of America

Design by M.R.P. Design
Typesetting and composition by Sam Sheng, CompuDesign

10 9 8 7 6 5 4 3 2

Library of Congress Cataloging-in-Publication Data

Basnight, Bobby.
     What ship is that? / written and illustrated by Bobby L. Basnight.
          p.   cm.
       ISBN 1-55821-433-X
       1. Ships—Recognition.   I. Title.
     VM307.B34   1996
     623.8'2—dc20
                                                                    96-15827
                                                                    CIP

CONTENTS

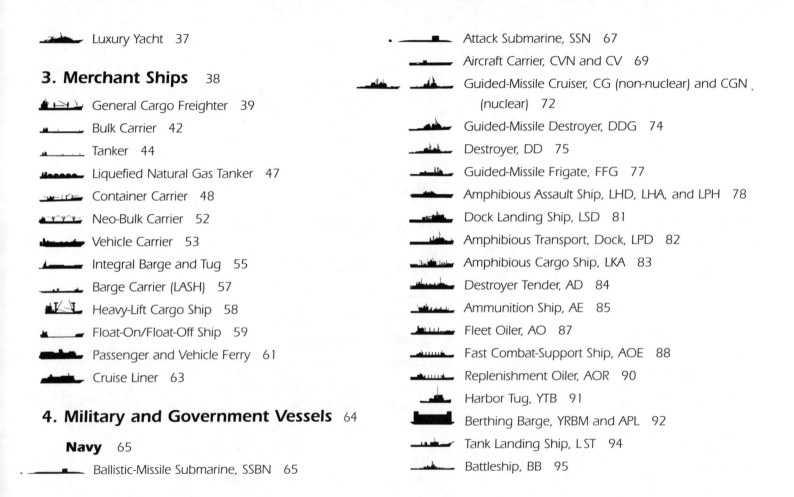

ACKNOWLEDGMENTS

I'd like to thank the following for their contributions to this project:

Shirley Basnight

James R. Babb

James P. Goodwin Jr.

Charles Meade Amory

Tom and Selina Stokes

Randy Stokes

Oscar Lind

Peter Bragg, *Master Chief U.S. Navy, ret.*

Commander H. Collins Embry, *U.S. Navy, ret.*

Thomas Vodicka, *Maritime Administration*

Isaac Harter III

William H. Wilson

Colonna's Shipyard, *Norfolk, VA*

Campbell Shipyard, *San Diego, CA*

U.S. Army Transportation Center, *Fort Eustus, Public Affairs*

Department of the Navy, *Office of Information*

U.S. Coast Guard, *Public Affairs, Washington & Yorktown*

National Oceanic and Atmospheric Administration

AMPRO Fisheries, *Reedville, VA*

MARCO Marine Construction & Design, *Seattle, WA*

Alaska Department of Fish and Game

International Pacific Halibut Commission

U.S. Department of Transportation, *James River Reserve Fleet*

INTRODUCTION

What is it about a ship that stirs our imagination and makes us long for faraway places? Why should an obscure shape looming out of the fog provoke curiosity, then the vague feeling that our existence is too dull, too safe, too predictable?

Like ships, the towering buildings of great cities change hue and texture when washed by sunlight or rain; they're packed with activity and drama, and their lofty spires disappear into the fog. But a provincial traveler who stands in awe of skyscrapers one day may be comfortably employed in a top-floor office the next. The transition to the bridge of a naval vessel or even a harbor tug is far less easily accomplished, or even imagined.

Trains and aircraft have their own lore and devotees, but both are familiar, accessible; to go aboard, you need only buy a ticket. With the exception of ferries and cruise ships, buying a ticket will rarely take you to sea. Aircraft and trains follow schedules, arriving at the same time at the same place each day. A ship is more elusive, arriving unannounced, appearing suddenly. Twenty minutes ago she was over the horizon, obscured by fog or the night. Now something awesome in size has materialized, seemingly from nowhere.

How do you become part of this strange environment of ships and the sea, a world so poetic at a distance yet so vividly real and rusty up close? I hope this book is a start. "What Ship Is That?" is the age-old hail between skippers meeting at sea, and I can think of no better title for a book that aspires to help you peel away a bit of fog from the unknown. It assumes your previous encounters with the maritime world amount to little more than watching the movie *Sand Pebbles* or a TV rerun of *Victory At Sea*. It requires from you only curiosity.

Perhaps you've strolled onto an oceanfront boardwalk, where the shock of salt spray hurled at you by half a gale urged you to seek shelter. Instead you stopped and wondered about those slow-moving gray forms on the horizon. Where are they going? Who lives aboard them? What are they carrying? Why are they out in this lousy weather?

Maybe you're visiting a port city for the first time, and your hotel window reveals a grand, panoramic view of a busy harbor cluttered with tugs, barges, and a myriad of vessels in a seemingly infinite variety of sizes and shapes, some bearing little resemblance to anything you recognize as a ship.

I'll try to sort through some of this confusion, at least enough to allow you to announce confidently at dinner that you saw a nuclear aircraft carrier slipping down-channel, or a thousand-foot oil tanker lying empty at anchor, waiting for a cargo. I'll avoid the technical in favor of general information about ships and their identification, and provide some tips that will enable a dockside observer to interpret the show being played offshore.

Even a far-off ship at anchor reveals signs of activity, clues to her immediate status, some hint of the business at hand: loading galley stores, or waiting for a harbor pilot or tugs, or for her turn at the pier. There will be smoke, steam, lights, discharge water, flag signals—each providing material for a one-page sea story.

A vessel may even appear to be a rustbucket, neglected or abandoned, while her dented and paint-flecked hull is concealing the smells of good food, a humming electrical generator, an on-line boiler that could be brought up to steaming capacity within the hour.

Identifying individual ships by name, owner, or nationality is beyond the scope of this book. Indeed, such an endeavor is almost beyond the ability of specialists in the field; the maritime world, no pun intended, is just too fluid. Around the globe ships are sliding off builders' ways at about the same rate they're being towed to ship-breakers' yards. Merchant ships change owners, names, and flags— sometimes while at sea—to accommodate the rise and fall of commodity markets, to adjust to changes of governments,

to profit from or avoid wars. Their masts and cranes are frequently modified to handle new types of cargo, or to suit the loading and unloading facilities of new ports in emerging countries. Sometimes they're cut in half and "jumbo-ized," increasing the length of the carrying space.

Such activity makes it impossible for a "spotter's guide" to nail down specifics; we can only go for broad groups of vessels, trying to arrange them in categories based upon their general purpose, and upon their typical hull and superstructure characteristics. Too bad ships aren't as reasonable and consistent as fish or birds, and don't hold still in their evolution long enough for us to prepare a definitive handbook.

Regardless of how bizarre her shape, or how awkward or ungainly a ship may appear, some fundamental elements are always present. She must be inherently stable—able to regain an upright position after each blow from the sea and wind. She must keep the water outside, and her internal structure of frames, beams, longitudinals, bulkheads, decks, and keel must be so integrated that she's capable of absorbing all of the loads and forces nature will surely toss at her.

To achieve such design requirements, the vessel must have many external features common to all ships, from sailing vessels to the latest nuclear-powered warships. I'll use these features as "thumbnail" silhouettes, page-markers that should help you quickly categorize an unknown ship. Each ship is first of all a hull that must meet the dynamic demands of the sea; special superstructures, housings, riggings, and guns are then added to enable her to carry out her task.

Watching ships is a little like having a front-row seat at the longest-running play in town. Trains, automobiles, and aircraft are recent comers. The drama at sea has been unfolding for centuries. One ship's life span overlaps another's, all the way back to hollowed logs. Such historic events as the Spanish Armada's journey up the English Channel, the British victory at Trafalgar, the Union's blockade of the Confederate South, the sinking of the *Titanic,* and the invasion of Normandy are all linked directly to the vessels you see in today's harbors, in an unbroken evolutionary trail.

Shipbuilding did not take a quantum leap into the future with the introduction of nuclear power, leaving all empirical data obsolete. The atomic reactor is just another way to boil water. The rest of a nuclear vessel's machinery is essentially the same as any conventional steamship's.

It's been said that if you're writing a man's biography, get him out of short pants in the first chapter. I feel the same about nautical history. Most works fill too many beginning pages with woodcuts of ancient galleys and scenes of straw boats from Egyptian tombs. But this is a ship-spotter's guide, and you can't spot her if she's gone. However, some ships are only recently gone, and others may be resurrected. The battleship has exited the stage several times but keeps getting called back. A surviving J-boat, a real dinosaur from the opulent years of yacht-racing, has returned in all her original splendor. And recurring energy crises cyclically rekindle interest in the square-rigged, steel-hull nitrate ships of the recent past. Take a look at the *Peking* if you're down on South Street in Manhattan. Dressed up and trimmed out in today's technology, there may well be unexplored potential for a modern wind-ship.

Keep in mind that there's more to this ship-spotting business than just ticking them off as you spot them. Sometimes it starts off that way, and then you find there's something grand going on—an interplay of humanity and weather, market supply and demand, the need to maintain order, to catch fish, to win a race. Even if you're stuck on the shore you can enjoy it, become a part of it.

So tuck this little book into your rucksack, along with a camera and a pair of binoculars, and you may discover sea yarns of your own.

A SHIP-SPOTTER'S GUIDE

Faced with an unknown ship, you may find it convenient to "size her up" by locating on her the features common to most boats and ships. These components are dictated first by the demands of naval architecture and of the sea, and second by the job the ship is designed to perform. Sometimes tack-on features are added for the sake of style.

Before you thumb through the following pages, here are a few tips that will help you quickly find the relevant section. The vessels are grouped into categories: harbor, merchant, government, fishing, sail, and river. The problem is, the categorical distinctions are often blurred. Size alone won't distinguish them; some ships are dual-purpose, and few have a unique identifying feature. Masting and rigging are a jumble of contradictions in sailing ships, and serve a variety of purposes in merchant ships.

Don't mistake a stack of shipping containers for a deckhouse. I've omitted shipping containers from the identification silhouettes. If you suspect a shape may be a ship structure but notice that it's quilted and patched with long rectangular swatches of pale blues and reddish browns, assume it's a stack of containers.

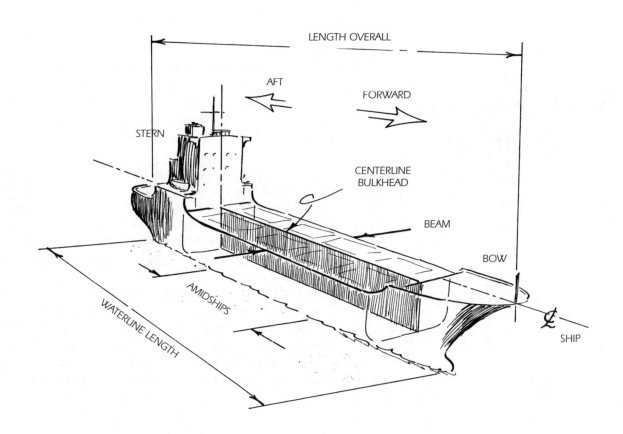

LENGTH OVERALL

AFT

FORWARD

STERN

CENTERLINE
BULKHEAD

BEAM

BOW

AMIDSHIPS

WATERLINE LENGTH

₡
SHIP

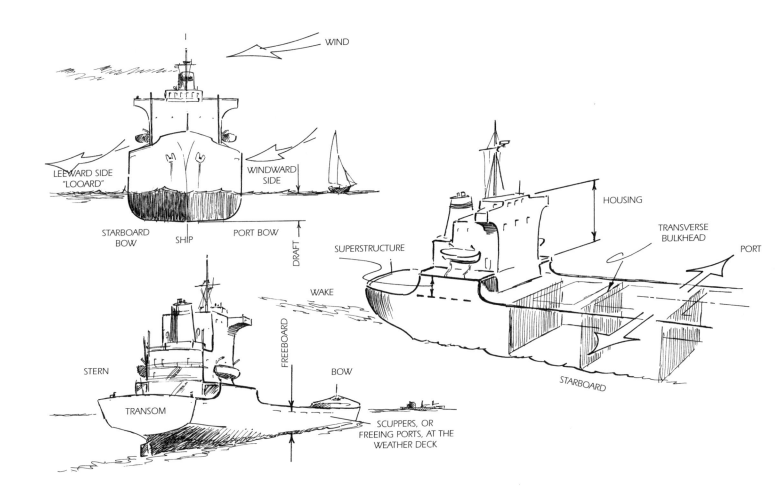

WIND

LEEWARD SIDE
"LOOARD"

WINDWARD
SIDE

STARBOARD
BOW

SHIP

PORT BOW

DRAFT

HOUSING

TRANSVERSE
BULKHEAD

PORT

SUPERSTRUCTURE

STARBOARD

WAKE

STERN

FREEBOARD

BOW

TRANSOM

SCUPPERS, OR
FREEING PORTS, AT THE
WEATHER DECK

STEP ONE: SHEER

For the would-be identifier of ships, the sheer line is the defining characteristic but also the most difficult to define, because it involves a mixture of art and science, practicality and aesthetics.

The classic sheer starts at the top of the bow stem, then sweeps aft in a long, downward curve to a point approximately three-quarters of the way back from the stem, from which it sweeps upward to meet the top of the transom. The problem is, a lot of curves fit within those three points. Most naval architects agree about the structural integrity introduced by the sheer line, but few agree about what is pleasing or graceful in its appearance. These days, pleasure and grace are given little weight in the design of ships. The bottom line is profit; beauty is a happy spin-off.

When builders worked in wood, limitations were imposed by the material; the working and shaping of wood led to natural, pleasing curves. Substantial sheer had to be built into a wooden hull to prevent the ship from sagging at each end. A useful fringe benefit of this was the low free-board it created at the turn of the sheer, which made it much easier to work over the ship's side when hauling aboard nets, or anything else.

Modern technology and materials have pretty much eliminated the need for a pronounced sheer, and in most ships today the sheer is a straight line. No real problem with that; a straight line does not offend the eye.

The top edge of the hull is the sheer line, but in some ships there's no indication of where the hull starts and the other superstructure stops, and you may have to estimate the sheer from a continuous weld seam or a line of portholes. You may even choose the rail of the lowest weather deck and mentally extend that line to the bow and stern. Note, for identification, if there are decks above your extended sheer line. Is there a forecastle deck forward; a bridge deck amidships; or a poop deck aft?

What you're trying to develop is an "eye" for the basic shape of the hull portion of the black silhouette printed in the corner of these pages. This is the first step in identifying that strange shape anchored a mile out in the bay.

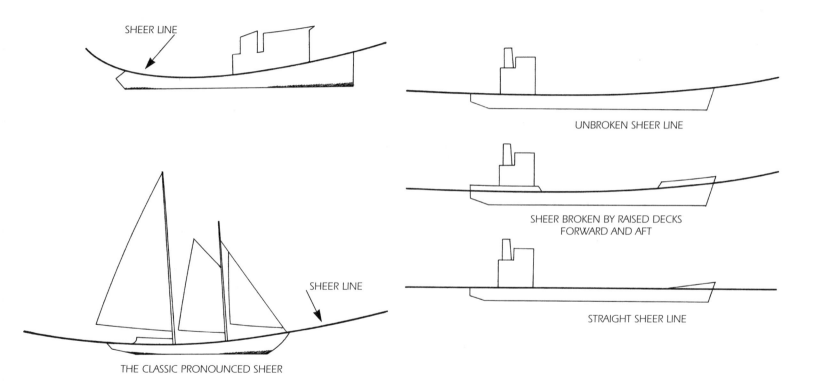

SHEER LINE

UNBROKEN SHEER LINE

SHEER BROKEN BY RAISED DECKS
FORWARD AND AFT

SHEER LINE

STRAIGHT SHEER LINE

THE CLASSIC PRONOUNCED SHEER

STEP TWO: BOWS AND STERNS

Next, turn your attention to the shapes of the bow and stern. Bows are designed with a number of objectives in mind, according to the intended purpose of the ship and the waters she will frequent. All that flare and rake, so stylish on yachts and cruise ships, is a fortunate result of the need to provide the ship with "reserve buoyancy"—extra inside volume that enhances the bow's resistance to being pushed underwater by wind, sea, and the ship's own power. Building in extra volume with flared sides and a forward rake provides both reserve buoyancy and pleasing angles and curves. Yacht designers may exaggerate the ship's lines for style beyond what is necessary to assure proper buoyancy and stability.

The need to handle cargo or fishing gear over the stern naturally influences the shape of the stern, as well as increasing the need for reserve buoyancy. In working vessels, little is arbitrary in the construction of bows and sterns.

An exception is the raked-forward transom found on many current sailing boats, which gives up valuable deck space for the sake of style. The trend started when the designers of a 12-meter racing sloop sliced off a diagonal chunk from the stern, from deck to waterline, to save weight without being penalized by yacht-rating rules based on waterline length. A legitimate reason indeed, since her job was to win races. Soon, admen and bean counters had incorporated this feature into the shape of ordinary daysailers. I mean, if a 12-meter racer has it, then this generic Clorox bottle must go like smoke!

If you're certain you've identified the hull type correctly, but the ship you see seems much lower or higher in the water than this book's silhouette, the ship may be sailing loaded to capacity, or totally empty and with little or no ballast.

Should all the components of your ship correspond with a silhouette but she appears to be shorter, she may be steering slightly away from you, or toward you. A foreshortened perspective will lessen apparent length.

BOWS

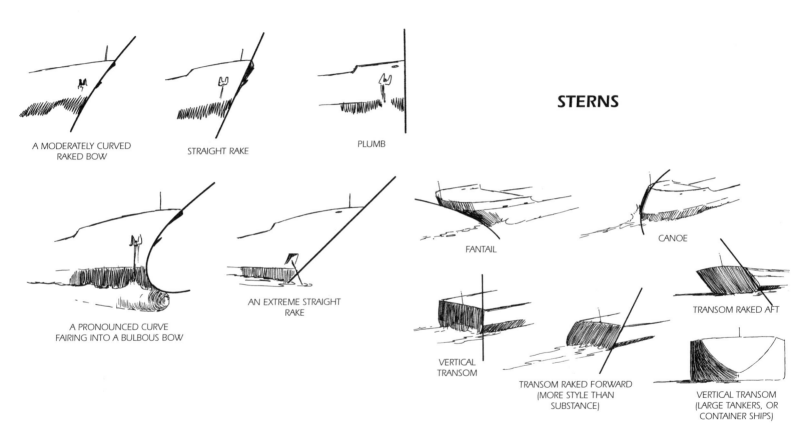

A MODERATELY CURVED
RAKED BOW

STRAIGHT RAKE

PLUMB

STERNS

A PRONOUNCED CURVE
FAIRING INTO A BULBOUS BOW

AN EXTREME STRAIGHT
RAKE

FANTAIL

CANOE

VERTICAL
TRANSOM

TRANSOM RAKED FORWARD
(MORE STYLE THAN
SUBSTANCE)

TRANSOM RAKED AFT

VERTICAL TRANSOM
(LARGE TANKERS, OR
CONTAINER SHIPS)

STEP THREE: LOCATION OF DECKHOUSING, SUPERSTRUCTURE, AND STACK

Where's the stack? This is a quick reference for classifying a ship by job or purpose. I wish I could give you some hard-and-fast rules that would positively define ship types based on appearances, but ships just won't obey rules. Let's say that, from years of observation, a specific seabird is known to be a fish-eater. Since the beginning of time, no one has ever seen this bird eat anything but fish. Print this fact in a bird book, however, and next week one will be seen in the parking lot of a fast-food restaurant having a go at a cheeseburger.

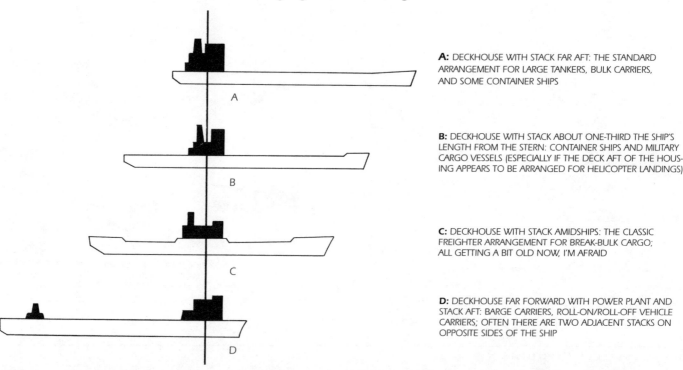

A: DECKHOUSE WITH STACK FAR AFT: THE STANDARD ARRANGEMENT FOR LARGE TANKERS, BULK CARRIERS, AND SOME CONTAINER SHIPS

B: DECKHOUSE WITH STACK ABOUT ONE-THIRD THE SHIP'S LENGTH FROM THE STERN: CONTAINER SHIPS AND MILITARY CARGO VESSELS (ESPECIALLY IF THE DECK AFT OF THE HOUSING APPEARS TO BE ARRANGED FOR HELICOPTER LANDINGS)

C: DECKHOUSE WITH STACK AMIDSHIPS: THE CLASSIC FREIGHTER ARRANGEMENT FOR BREAK-BULK CARGO; ALL GETTING A BIT OLD NOW, I'M AFRAID

D: DECKHOUSE FAR FORWARD WITH POWER PLANT AND STACK AFT: BARGE CARRIERS, ROLL-ON/ROLL-OFF VEHICLE CARRIERS; OFTEN THERE ARE TWO ADJACENT STACKS ON OPPOSITE SIDES OF THE SHIP

STEP FOUR: CARGO-HANDLING GEAR

Using the stack as a reference marker, divide the ship into two sections. Count the number of cargo masts, or cranes, installed on the forward section, and the number installed on the aft section. Dividing the ship into two parts this way is only a mental filing tab to enable you to keep in mind the placement of the gear. There are no hard-and-fast rules governing the numerical distribution of masts or cranes.

Check the ship silhouettes for the same or similar configuration of rigging.

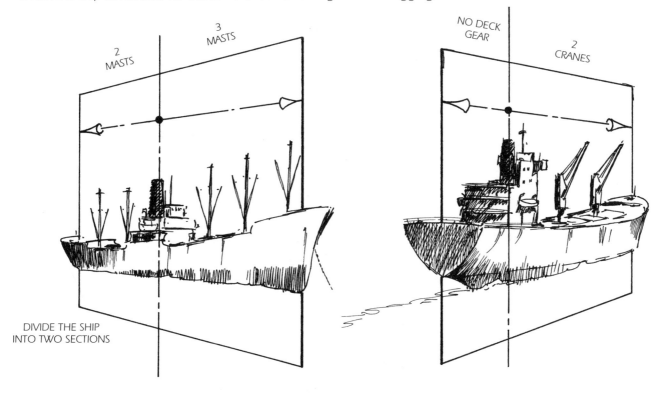

3 MASTS

2 MASTS

NO DECK GEAR

2 CRANES

DIVIDE THE SHIP INTO TWO SECTIONS

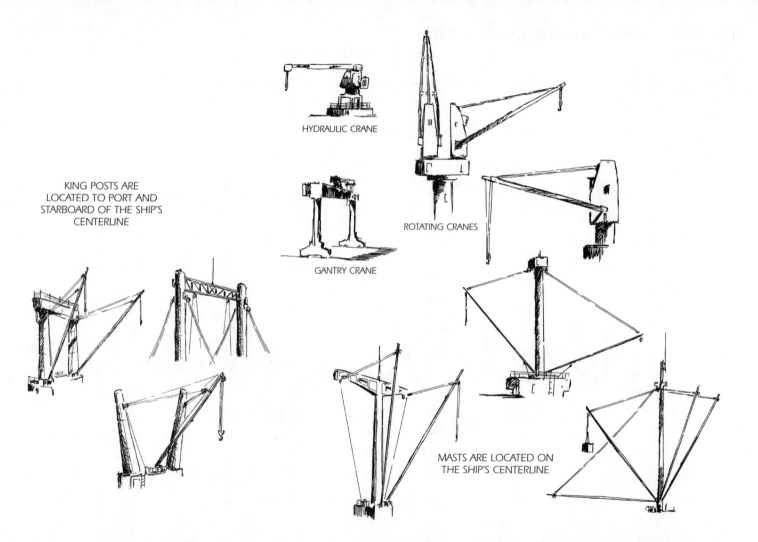

HYDRAULIC CRANE

KING POSTS ARE
LOCATED TO PORT AND
STARBOARD OF THE SHIP'S
CENTERLINE

ROTATING CRANES

GANTRY CRANE

MASTS ARE LOCATED ON
THE SHIP'S CENTERLINE

MILITARY SHIPS

Most navies of the world paint their ships gray; a few naval-support ships are painted white. Most have big white numbers on the bow, outlined with a black shadow. These days, conventional guns are small, and missile-launching stands are inconspicuous.

The navy classifies its ships and small vessels with abbreviations that do not always have an apparent meaning to civilians. CV for carrier vessel or CVN for carrier vessel (nuclear) is pretty obvious, but LKA for an amphibious cargo ship or YTB for a harbor tug does not really identify the type of vessel to one unfamiliar with the nomenclature. A few designators are absolute: If the basic abbreviation has a "T" prefix, the ship belongs to the Military Sealift Command or is under the administration of the Ready Reserve Force. If there is a "W" prefix, she is the property of the United States Coast Guard. Another reason for the selection of a particular abbreviation may be to avoid confusion and mistakes in message transmissions and correspondence.

The terms are readily used within the services; a sailor is more likely to say he is stationed on an AD, rather than aboard a destroyer tender.

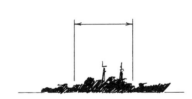

ON WARSHIPS, THE BULK OF THE HOUSING AND SUPERSTRUCTURE MAY BE LOCATED AMIDSHIPS, AWAY FROM THE BOW AND STERN

MASTS ON MILITARY SHIPS ARE CROWDED WITH RADAR AND COMMUNICATIONS ANTENNA

5" LIGHTWEIGHT GUN

PHALANX CLOSE-IN WEAPONS SYSTEM (CIWS)

If the height of your eye above sea level is	The distance to the horizon is
5 feet	2.9 miles
10 feet	4.2 miles
15 feet	5.1 miles
20 feet	5.9 miles
50 feet	9.3 miles
100 feet	13.2 miles

If the ship is closer to you than the horizon, you'll see all of her. If she's farther away than the horizon, you will begin to see less.

THE HORIZON

What you may think is a deeply loaded tanker could in fact be the upper parts of a ship just over the horizon. With your feet on the sand at the edge of the sea, the distance to the visible horizon (depending on your height) is about three miles. Any ship beyond that distance will begin to drop below your horizon due to the curvature of the earth. Standing at sea level, you may only see a portion of a ship's hull, or just the stack and masts (the ship is said to be **hull down**). Look at the same ship from your hotel balcony and you'll see the whole ship. You're probably thinking that this is elementary stuff, so why is he wasting my time?

Thinking about the horizon has little place in our present civilization; we no longer scan the horizon, watching for the approach of enemies, as did our ancestors. Some behavioral scientists claim, however, that a modern businessman, having lunch in the heart of the financial district, will, after the second bite of his chop, scan the room in a 180-degree arc at the level the horizon would be were he back in the bush.

"A"

HORIZON FOR "A"

HORIZON FOR "B"

SHIP AS SEEN BY "A"

SHIP AS SEEN BY "B"

THE PLIMSOLL MARK

Admiralty laws regulate the amount of cargo a ship may carry, depending upon the time of year and the waters of operation. Their intent is to maintain enough reserve buoyancy and a low enough center of gravity to ensure the safety of the ship in adverse weather and in dangerous seas.

By reading her Plimsoll marks, you can determine at a glance if a ship is empty or "loaded to her marks." The marks are often obscured by streaks of coal, cement dust, or rust.

Ships expecting to trade worldwide are marked for tropical fresh water, fresh water, tropical seawater, summer seawater, winter seawater, and—most ominous of all—winter North Atlantic. The circle-crossed-with-a-bar is a quick reference mark that's level with the summer seawater bar.

The shaded areas are spaces for paying cargo; the remaining space houses the ship's main and auxiliary machinery, living spaces, and supply lockers. A businessman may look at these areas as earning space, as opposed to overhead. Cargo weight to ship weight, fuel consumed to miles sailed, cubic feet filled with birdseed as opposed to bathtubs—there's a lot of work here for home-office statisticians and bookkeepers.

Vessels without cargo are often extremely unstable, and must take in water ballast to maintain a low center of gravity and a proper fore-and-aft trim. Sailing ships used stones for ballast. Discarded ballast from sailing vessels provided material for the cobblestone streets still found at old commercial waterfronts.

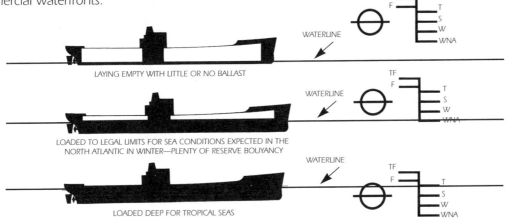

LAYING EMPTY WITH LITTLE OR NO BALLAST

LOADED TO LEGAL LIMITS FOR SEA CONDITIONS EXPECTED IN THE NORTH ATLANTIC IN WINTER—PLENTY OF RESERVE BUOYANCY

LOADED DEEP FOR TROPICAL SEAS

A Brief Note on Funnel, or Stack, Markings

Stack markings come and go with some frequency, prompted by changes of ownership or responsible agency. Often, repainting the stack doesn't even keep up with the legal transactions. New markings are seen without introduction, and old ones fade away without explanation.

Unlike military ships, there's little order in the use of colors or designs on the stacks of merchant ships. Merchant markings are of all colors, or combinations of colors, with smart logos of the type seen on banks and gas stations. Most are designed by ad agencies; others, I suspect, by the owner's brother-in-law. Private colors may establish ownership, but are of little use in identifying ship types.

American naval surface ships have solid gray stacks, sometimes topped with black to hide the soot stains from the boiler smoke or engine exhaust.

Military Sealift Command ships (naval ships crewed by civilians) can be identified by their horizontal bands of black, gray,

(continued on page 15)

AN ELEVATION DRAWING OF A C5 FREIGHTER

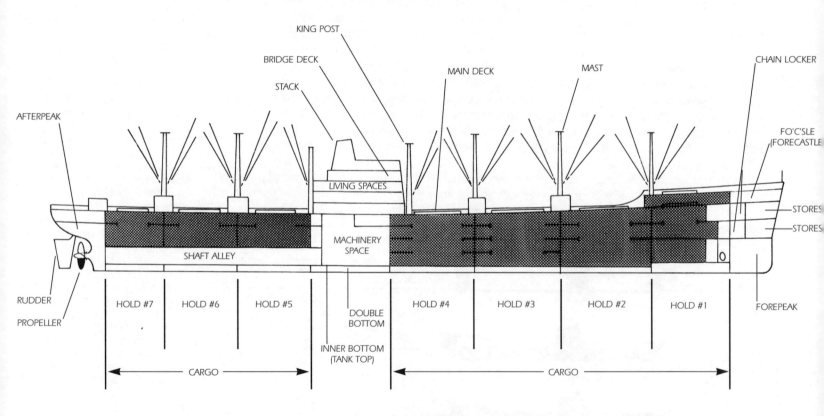

KING POST

BRIDGE DECK

STACK

MAIN DECK

MAST

CHAIN LOCKER

AFTERPEAK

FO'C'SLE (FORECASTLE)

LIVING SPACES

MACHINERY SPACE

SHAFT ALLEY

STORES

STORES

RUDDER

PROPELLER

HOLD #7

HOLD #6

HOLD #5

DOUBLE BOTTOM

INNER BOTTOM (TANK TOP)

HOLD #4

HOLD #3

HOLD #2

HOLD #1

FOREPEAK

CARGO

CARGO

A REFERENCE SCALE

1. A tractor-trailer with a 40-foot shipping container is used for vessels over 200 feet long.
2. A man rowing a 12-foot dory is used for vessels under 200 feet long.
3. Vessels under 200 feet may feature a 6-foot crew member in the sketch.

(continued from page 13)

blue, and gold. The Ready Reserve Force (cargo vessels maintained by the United States Maritime Administration) have red, white, and blue horizontal bands.

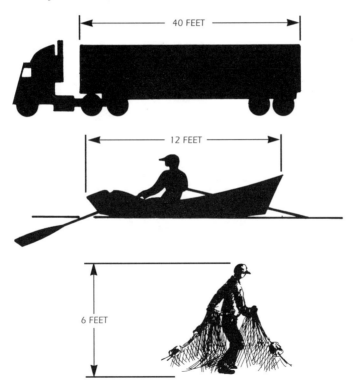

40 FEET

12 FEET

6 FEET

TWO SHIPS OBSERVED FROM POSITIONS A, B, AND C

Two vessels at anchor, several miles from the observer, may present misleading silhouettes, especially if the atmosphere is hazy. An observer at point **A** could assume he was seeing a large roll-on/roll-off ship with two adjacent stacks aft. If he moved on to point **B,** he might begin to think the ship was some sort of barge carrier. Only from point **C** do the two ships separate and present a true view of the situation.

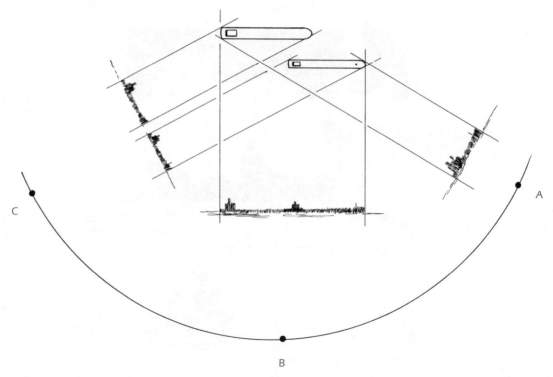

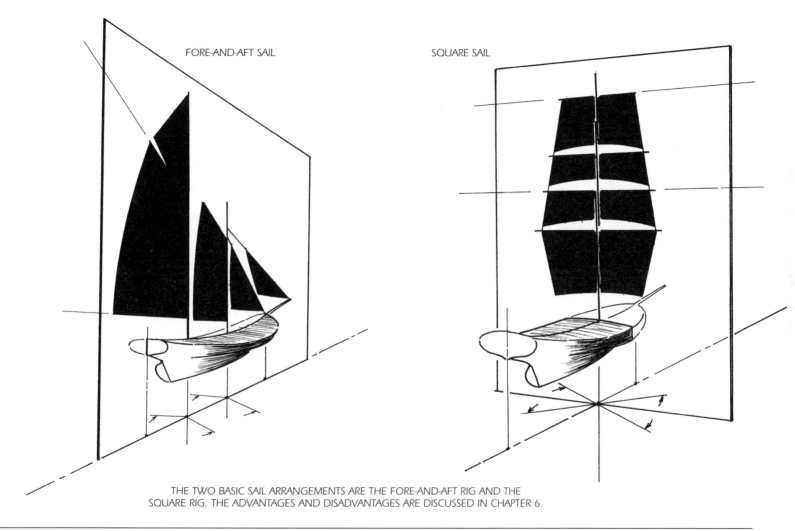

FORE-AND-AFT SAIL

SQUARE SAIL

THE TWO BASIC SAIL ARRANGEMENTS ARE THE FORE-AND-AFT RIG AND THE
SQUARE RIG. THE ADVANTAGES AND DISADVANTAGES ARE DISCUSSED IN CHAPTER 6.

SIGNAL FLAGS

All communication between ships is now conducted by radio; it's unlikely that you'll see any merchant ships flying signal flags. The military still has a go at it now and then—just for drill, I suspect. If you see what appears to be the entire alphabet hanging from a line rigged from the bow stem to the masthead and down to the stern, you're probably seeing holiday decorations. Meaningful signals are in code, and generally use only one to three flags.

In addition to the single-flag codes, there are hundreds of two- and three-flag codes covering any conceivable situation likely to arise in routine ship-handling. The list of available messages covers casualties and damages, navigation, maneuvers, weather, medical emergencies, and distress and other nonmedical emergencies.

Certainly, radio communication has eliminated misinterpreted codes and mistaken identification of flags resulting from distance and weather. Now ship captains, pilots, bridge-tenders, tug skippers, and even aircraft are all tied together in a radio communication network that can be used to coordinate movements of ships and services. If the International Code of Signals had any advantage over radio, it was in overcoming language barriers and accents. Each captain had a copy of the codebook in the language he could understand.

The codes range from the ordinary affairs of shipping—**SU 1,** "My cargo is coal"—to the dramatic **SQ 1,** "Stop or heave to, otherwise I shall open fire on you." Today, an inbound ship's captain can arrange for a pilot by radio hours in advance of his arrival off the sea buoy; however, the **G** flag, requesting a pilot, and the **H** flag, informing anyone concerned that a pilot is aboard, must still be shown by law. Another required flag is the **Q** signal, requesting clearance from the port's health authority to enter the harbor.

An old chum of mine, who owned a very small yacht, was more attentive to the proper display of code flags than anyone else I ever knew, especially the codes from the medical chapter of the *International Code of Signals.* If his wife or kids had a cold, he felt it his duty to warn visitors of the contagious viruses aboard by flying the **MIC,** "Patient has severe cough," or the **MHL,** "Throat is sore and red." His family felt that literally hanging their personal medical record out on a line was carrying protocol to the extreme. However, I must give him credit for applying the rules equally to himself. After a night of partying, during which a sizable quantity of imported Dutch beer was consumed, he ran up his own diagnosis: **MJV**, "Patient is unable to hold urine."

The signals most likely to be used routinely, or used in emergencies, have been assigned a single letter and are listed on the next page. A complete list of signals and the proper procedures for signaling is found in the *International Code of Signals, United States Edition,* Pub. 102. There you can find all of the combinations of letters and numbers that form the hundreds of messages necessary to communicate your intentions, or ask questions, for most any situation arising at sea.

26 SIGNALS:

A: I have a diver down; keep well clear at slow speed.

B: I am taking in, or discharging, or carrying dangerous goods.

C: Yes.

D: Keep clear of me; I am maneuvering with difficulty.

E: I am altering my course to starboard.

F: I am disabled; communicate with me.

G: I require a pilot. [When made by a fishing vessel operating on or close to fishing grounds] I am hauling nets.

H: I have a pilot on board.

I: I am altering my course to port.

J: I am on fire and have dangerous cargo on board; keep clear of me.

K: I wish to communicate with you.

L: You should stop your vessel instantly.

M: My vessel is stopped and making no way through the water.

N: No.

O: Man overboard.

P: [In harbor] All persons should report on board as the vessel is about to proceed to sea. [At sea, if used by fishing vessel] My nets have come fast upon an obstruction.

Q: My vessel is healthy and I request free pratique.

R: I have received your last signal.

S: My engines are going astern.

T: Keep clear of me; I am engaged in pair trawling.

U: You are running into danger.

V: I require assistance.

W: I require medical assistance.

X: Stop carrying out your intentions and watch for my signals.

Y: I am dragging my anchor.

Z: I require a tug. [When made by a fishing vessel operating on or close to fishing grounds] I am shooting nets.

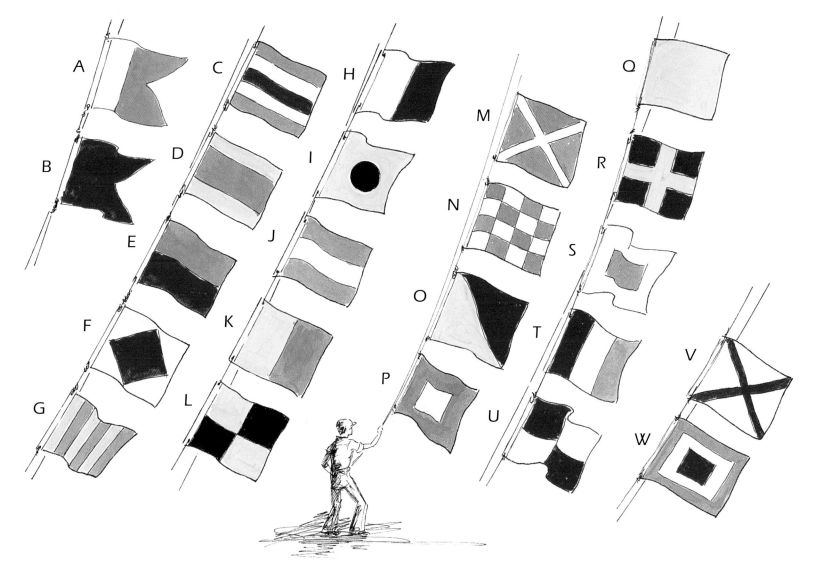

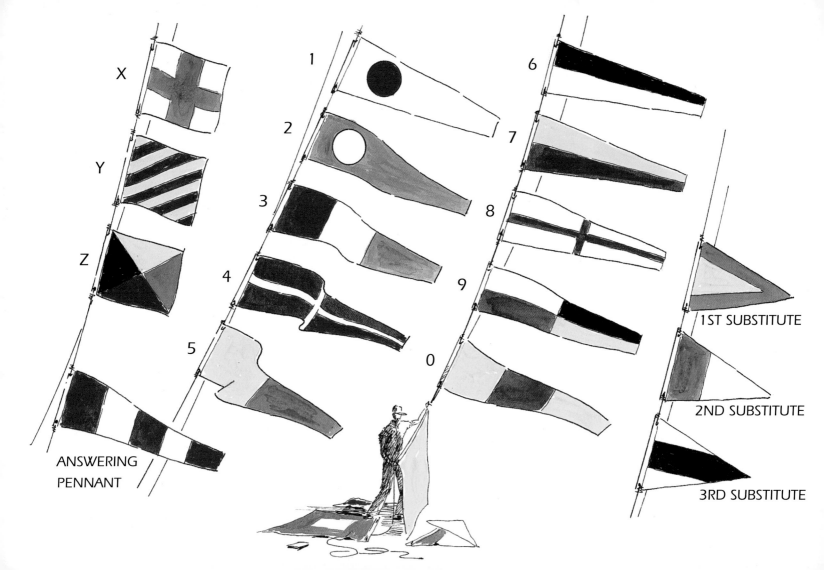

X

Y

Z

ANSWERING
PENNANT

1

2

3

4

5

6

7

8

9

0

1ST SUBSTITUTE

2ND SUBSTITUTE

3RD SUBSTITUTE

IN HARBOR

2

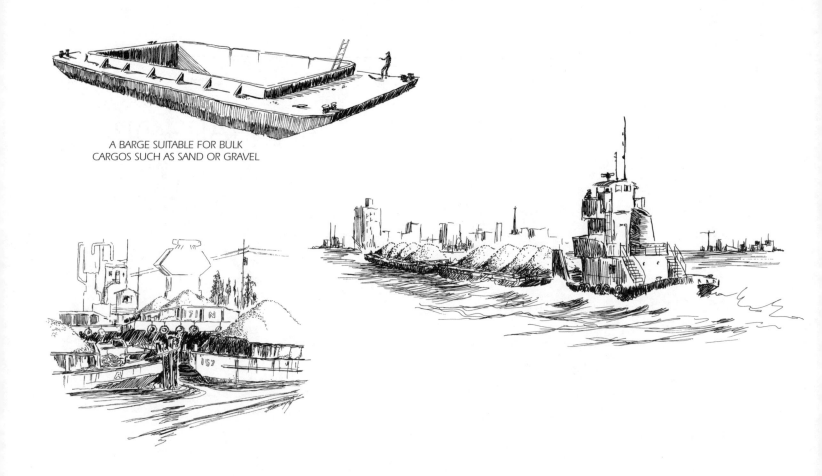

A BARGE SUITABLE FOR BULK
CARGOS SUCH AS SAND OR GRAVEL

WHAT SHIP IS THAT?

BARGE

A few barge types emerged from the early part of this century with a lasting identity, provoking nostalgia and inspiring watercolor artists—the Thames sailing barge, for instance, or those motorized French barges now converted into chic residences moored on the Seine. Few, if any, of today's working barges will enjoy a prestigious retirement, however. In the hierarchy of ships, barges are coolies.

The purpose of a barge is to carry large, heavy loads economically. It must be able to withstand sea conditions but at the same time have a minimum draft so that, if necessary, it can be taken into shallow waters to discharge cargo directly to a receiver. The structural requirements are simple: A barge must be strong enough to absorb the shock from loads dropped by crane operators with poor depth perception, or from tug skippers depending upon steel bulkheads or other barges to stop their momentum. Barges must be able to survive sinking, collision, beaching, fire, and everything toxic, and be able to suffer less damage than they inflict while spending a three-day northeaster banging about beneath a highway bridge.

The majority of barges you will see in a harbor are flat-bottomed, with only a small deck around the sides and ends; these are most often used for transporting sand or gravel. Others have flush decks, used as construction platforms or for cargo that can be rolled on and off. You can identify tanker barges by the deck piping and pump house; sometimes, too, they fly a red flag. The size of a barge depends on where it'll be used. Inland waterway barges are limited by the depth and width of canals or locks; others are designed to fit aboard barge-carrying ships.

Barges are useful because the turnaround time required to load and unload them is brief, and so does not tie up a power vessel that could be earning money elsewhere. Barges employed in off-loading anchored ships are often referred to as **lighters.**

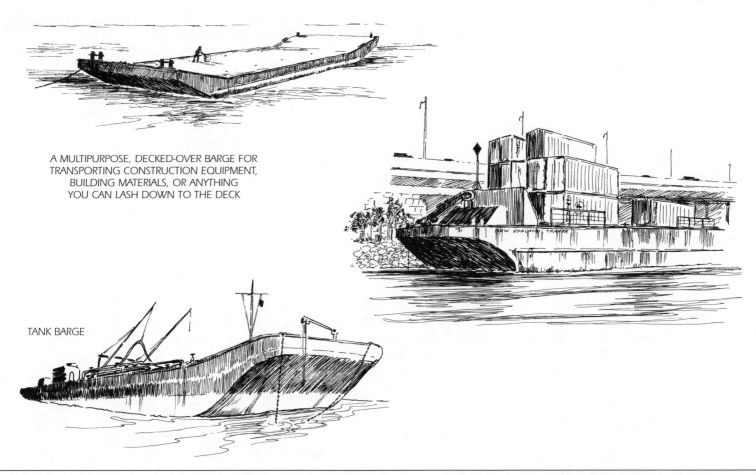

A MULTIPURPOSE, DECKED-OVER BARGE FOR
TRANSPORTING CONSTRUCTION EQUIPMENT,
BUILDING MATERIALS, OR ANYTHING
YOU CAN LASH DOWN TO THE DECK

TANK BARGE

SMALL PUSH-TYPE TUG

Tugs as small as 30 to 35 feet are most often owned by shipyards, railways, or other waterfront industries that need to move barges and vessels within their own docks and piers. With blunt bows, rigged with knees for pushing, and drawing as little as five feet of water, they are ideally suited for barge work on the inland waterway or freshwater rivers. A typical cargo might be one barge loaded with sand and gravel consigned to a cement plant in some headwater community.

The tugs are generally manned by a skipper and one deckhand. Should a second deckhand be employed, the first will promptly promote himself to "mate." On the water, the development of hierarchy starts early.

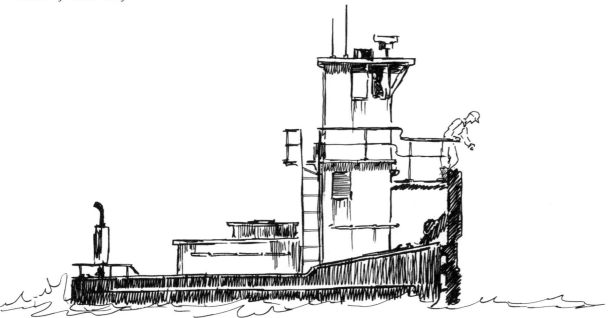

WHAT SHIP IS THAT?

LARGE PUSH-TYPE TUG

Looking very much like a large push-type river tug of the sort found on the Mississippi and other inland rivers, this vessel is seaworthy for work offshore or in exposed estuaries and bays. In profile, she appears to have a barge-bow, or scow-bow, but in fact has a conventional hull form that allows oceangoing voyages.

The hemp fenders and old tractor tires once used as protective cushions between tug and customer are giving way to custom-designed rubber bumpers. This is one of the few technical advances that are an aesthetic improvement over tradition.

HARBOR TUG

This is the classic tugboat, with a long, sweeping sheer ending low to the water; a squatty stern; a fat stack amidships with the company markings; and a black hull. The mast is hinged to allow snugging up under flared bows, and to prevent contact with overhanging sponsons or catwalks when the tug comes into close contact with hulls being pushed in and out of slips. A primary responsibility of harbor tugs is playing shepherd to arriving and departing ships. In some harbors, local laws require a tug to be present during docking operations, to prevent collisions.

For sailboat racers, tugs are an ever-present factor in navigation, to be evaluated along with wind shifts, currents, and shallow water. If your course appears to intersect with a tug's, it may be prudent to lose a few yards and cross in her wake.

An independent history of American towing companies would be an interesting account of fierce competition among dangerously serious rivals, engaged in a business with no rules and a slim margin for profit—a game played out by tough skippers and crews, and tight-fisted shipowners. This was a far different environment from that of the present towing business, inherited from the founders and now conducted from slick offices decorated with a few brass relics from long-departed tugs. Gone are the days of shouting from wheelhouse windows and pier-end dispatcher shacks. Major players today are linked by cellular phones and long-term contracts. Tug Boat Annie and her *Narcissus* disappeared with the *Saturday Evening Post*.

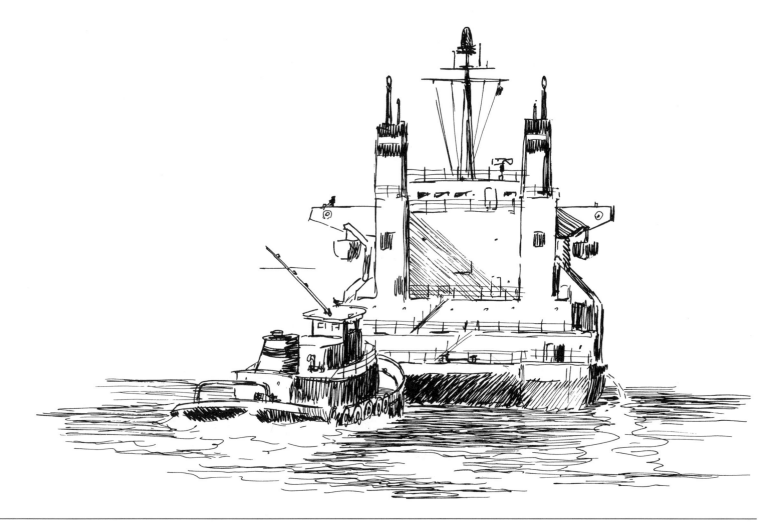

COASTAL and OCEANGOING TUG

A tug capable of ocean navigation is designed with greater seakeeping ability and more living facilities for the crew than those of a tug that works primarily in protected waters and harbors.

The enclosure perched high on a framework rising from the pilothouse roof is a secondary control station, allowing extended visibility above tall loads. Often, you'll see what appears to be a six-inch pipe arching across the deck at the stern from side to side. This is used to lift a sliding and shifting towing hawser over deck fittings that might otherwise entangle it.

There may or may not be a regular cook aboard; if not, the culinary job may be rotated among the regular crew. Honor and acclaim are frequently bestowed on the cooks of fishing vessels and logging camps; however, I've never heard of a great tugboat cook.

FLOATING DRY DOCK

Floating dry docks have many advantages over their excavated relatives. They're less expensive to build, they can be built far away from where they'll be used, and their operation doesn't require a shipyard to own land a thousand feet back from the water's edge. The principles behind a floating dry dock are simple: Open the air vents and let the water in until it sinks; position the ship inside the dry-dock walls; pump the water out of the dry dock until it floats. The ship, lightened of cargo, ballast, and fuel, will come up sitting high and dry on keel blocks.

When the deck of a dry dock rises above the water, there are often a few fish flapping about. I once informed a young engineer that it was a time-honored right of the shipyard's design department to have first dibs on all fish as soon as our dock was free of water. He looked skeptical. Later, when I returned from lunch, I presented him with a golden smoked whitefish from the local deli, and informed him it was his share. I apologized for there being only one fish, but, after all, he *was* the junior department member. The lad was horrified, his eyes filled with doubts over his choice of career and the cultural background of his new associates.

WHAT SHIP IS THAT?

FLOATING CRANE

You may never notice a floating crane—unless you spot one being towed in open water, separated from the clutter of industrial waterfronts. Floating cranes seem to spend a lot of time moored to piers, surrounded by an armada of decrepit barges and towboats and blending into the background. If its boom is in the upright position, you may mistake one for a shipyard crane. Its deck may be covered with the same litter of winches, vent ducts, welding equipment, oxygen tanks, cables, steel shapes, and pipes found on the adjacent pier. Often, a converted mobile home is aboard for a field office, serviced by a portable fiberglass latrine.

The purpose of a floating crane is to lift unusually heavy or awkward loads (such as prefabricated ship sections), or to reach into areas inaccessible to other, more conventional lift equipment. Barge cranes are indispensable tools in the construction of jetties, bridges, and bridge-tunnels—things that take years to build. There, too, the crane becomes part of the daily scene, on station for entire winters and summers, taken for granted as is any workhorse.

Their owners would be pleased if they were forever employed in scheduled work, but the public most appreciates floating cranes when they appear, almost overnight, on the site of some spectacular emergency, such as a collapsed bridge span or a vessel sunk in mid-channel. Released from a routine assignment or a long, idle layup, the floating crane is the only boy on the block that can put things right.

WHAT SHIP IS THAT?

RIVER FERRY

There are still a good number of small ferries in operation, mostly servicing remote communities without enough political influence in the statehouse to obtain funds for a bridge. When you're traveling, select a route with a ferry. There are good sounds involved: rattling chain falls, clanging steel ramps, roaring diesel engines, the squeaking of rubrails against creosoted pilings, and the clamor of seagulls fighting over minnows brought to the surface by the churning backwash of a propeller turning in reverse.

The capacities of river ferries vary from five to fifty automobiles. Most trips take about half an hour. You can review the road maps, get a diet cola from the drink machine, and talk to the nice person in the car up ahead.

SMALL TANKER, RIVERS and SOUNDS

The regions served by 100-foot tankers, transporting gasoline, diesel, and heating fuel, have diminished; they're mostly limited now to island communities. Those oil distributors who are fortunate enough to have a yard on a river or creek often own their own small tanker, or have one under contract to deliver oil products directly to them from the giant port terminals and tank farms. These tankers are the last water link between the refinery and the automobile or tractor.

A captain, a mate-engineer, and two deckhands pretty much round out the crew. Most voyages keep them away from home for only a few nights. Small inland tankers frequently serve areas far from cities and busy harbors, where the air and water are still pristine. They make their presence known by the smell of oil lingering in the atmosphere on hot, muggy days long after they've passed.

LUXURY YACHT

If she looks like she's moving fast even while at anchor; is gleaming white; has long rows of dark-tinted windows that you can't see through, along with white awnings, boarding ladders, swim platforms, and decks arranged with expensive-looking lawn furniture; and is flying no flag and displaying no markings—she's almost certainly a luxury yacht.

Should she be further trimmed out with a helicopter, tanned people with beautiful teeth, and perhaps a chap carrying a tray with pale green bottles, you can, with certainty, say you're looking at a luxury yacht that would do James Bond proud.

MERCHANT SHIPS

3

GENERAL CARGO FREIGHTER

A fine little ship—a bit under 300 feet and fitted out with her own cranes so she can load and unload in secondary ports with inadequate cargo-handling facilities—this vessel is a link between river and bay vessels and the larger ships that sail only between the world's major container terminals.

Her hatches are sized to accommodate standard shipping containers for stowage below, in the hold. She can carry another tier of containers on her weather deck. On a vessel of this size you'll likely find partial cargoes handled on pallets. These are loads too small to fill an entire container; they can be lifted aboard with a single spar boom.

No question, the shipping container reduces damage to cargo, eliminates pilferage by longshoremen, and expedites rapid rail or truck transportation to and from the docks; as usual, however, some things get lost in the quest for efficiency. Gone are the colors and smells of exotic commodities. Now it's only on smaller ships, such as this one, that you're likely to see 50-pound bags of coffee beans or a single Land Rover being swung aboard.

She has one diesel engine and probably keeps a crew of between eight and twelve. When I was a lad it was just such a vessel that I wanted to be captain of—a ship that might occasionally have the sea crossing her deck. I was raised on sea stories where the crew was always tumbling out the fo'c'sle door in the middle of the night, wearing sou'westers and sea boots, to wrestle with a deckload of 55-gallon drums of soft-drink syrup gone adrift. These days if you have to call out the off-duty watch you'll probably spend the morning filling out overtime forms.

This ship is small enough that you might see her hauled out on a railway for a routine overhaul; if so, you may be surprised to note how small her propeller is. Should you be observing from a harbor cruise boat, the stern is about all you'll see of her; however, if you have a view forward, note her bulbous bow—a trick of marine engineering that increases speed and fuel economy.

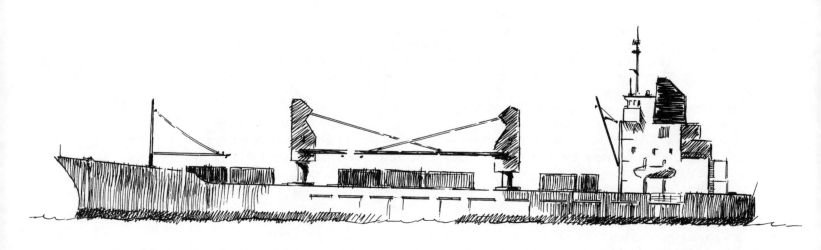

WHAT SHIP IS THAT?

BULK CARRIER

Sighted at sea, the bulk carrier presents the same profile as an oil tanker. Few have masts or cranes. Only a close observation of the deck reveals the distinction: The bulk carrier has evenly spaced hatch coamings; the tanker has clean decks with runs of exposed piping, manifolds, and valves.

In harbor a bulk carrier takes up a lot of space, and unless you have an unobstructed view you may think you're seeing two ships, or one with unidentifiable cargo-handling gear. A closer observation may reveal that a terminal building on a pier between you and the bulk carrier is blanking out a sizable portion of her middle and presenting you with the appearance of two ships. The strange deck gear may be a crane—located the equivalent of two city blocks from the water—being used to construct a new apartment building.

The cargo of a successfully employed bulk carrier rarely varies. She may sail for years between the same ports, engaged in the same work, under contract to the same supplier and purchaser. Bulk carriers in the regular coal or grain trade are single-purpose ships. Others, known as **OBOs** (ore, bulk, oil), are multipurpose, designed with a combination of dry space and tank arrangements to accommodate mixed cargoes.

TANKER

Hands down the largest ships ever built, tankers are controversial and dangerous, but when seen loaded to their marks and plowing into contrary seas, decks wet with spray, there's a terrible beauty about them. Small-boat sailors hold tankers in high regard. Regardless of good intentions on the part of the skipper or pilot on the tanker's bridge, there's little he can do to avoid collision with boats too suddenly placed in his path—especially in narrow channels.

Supertankers principally carry crude oil—direct from the drilling fields—and finished petroleum products. Smaller ships may be loaded with chlorine, turpentine, acids, formaldehyde, or any of a hundred different industrial chemicals—even molasses or wine.

Contrary to popular belief, tankers are safer when loaded. The danger of explosion comes after the cargo has been discharged, when the atmosphere inside the tanks can reach a critical mixture of volatile fumes and air. To prevent this, inert gases are introduced into the empty spaces to reduce the percentage of oxygen.

When an ore carrier sinks, ballads are written about the event. An overdue ship, and the implied widow staring out to sea, is the stuff of statues and paintings. A tanker disaster, however, does not inspire music or art. A schooner aground off Hatteras, her crew being taken off by the lifesaving service, inspires a painting. A photograph of a duck plastered with heavy crude inspires outrage and anger.

A tanker underway or anchored in an estuary presents the same profile as a bulk carrier. If instead of hatches you see piping laid out schematically on deck, she's a tanker. Of course, identification is much easier if the vessel is moored to a pier. Obviously, the tanker will be the ship you see at the refinery or tank terminal; the bulk carrier, near coal or ore conveyors, or grain elevators.

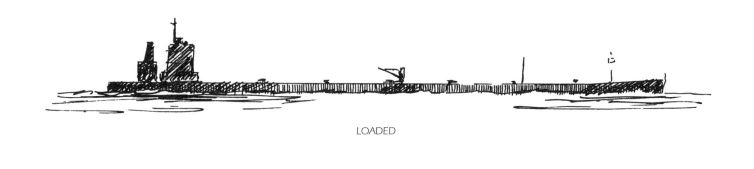

LOADED

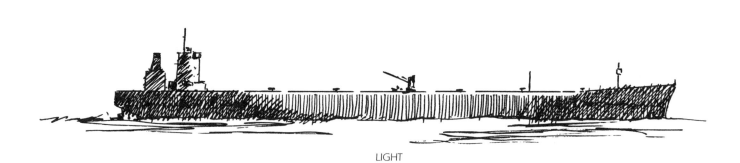

LIGHT

WHAT SHIP IS THAT?

LIQUEFIED NATURAL GAS TANKER

There's no mistaking this ship for any other. Spherical cargo tanks unquestionably establish her as an **LNG,** a liquefied natural gas tanker. Unlike an oil tanker, her profile will not change much when she's fully loaded. Even when compressed, the weight of the cargo is light in comparison to the space it occupies. The most awesome statistic relative to this ship is that her cargo may have a temperature of *minus* 255 degrees Fahrenheit.

CONTAINER CARRIER

When I was five years old, a dirigible passed low over our town—a *real* dirigible, not a blimp. It eclipsed the sun, and I was in its shadow. I ran inside. Years later, I had the same feeling when I sailed under the lee side of a giant container ship.

They materialize out of the fog like ragged islands. There's nothing graceful about them: no pleasing sheer, no low freeboard. Their impact comes from their boxy massiveness. There are longer ships—tankers and aircraft carriers—but on these, length is in proportion to height. A loaded container carrier may carry shipping containers stacked four or five tiers high the entire length of her weather deck, and she can have up to six layers of containers below.

There's no way to sketch a useful profile of a container carrier with a deck cargo. The only effect of a full cargo on most vessels is to settle them deeper into the water—sometimes cutting the height of the hull in half, but otherwise not changing the silhouette. Should the deckload of a container carrier be incomplete, with large gaps showing between stacks of shipping containers, she may appear to have additional housing, causing you to confuse her with a number of other categories of ships.

I ignored container carriers as subjects of paintings or sketches for some time. They were just too plain, with no complicated mazes of masts and rigging to enhance a sketch. Then I began to just appreciate their massiveness. Appearance notwithstanding, these ships are the latest step in the evolution of freight carriers, and are going about the world's work on a scale never before seen.

Every manufactured item imaginable is in those shipping containers—auto parts, gourmet foods, office furniture, lightbulbs, paint, coffee mugs, lawn mowers, hubcaps, waterbeds, vacuum cleaners, wallpaper, toys, fireworks, pottery, hot tubs, clothing, sausages—all safely protected from weather and theft, from the manufacturer right to the customer. Some shipping containers are humidity-controlled, others are refrigerated to carry meats, vegetables, and fruits grown on the other side of the globe.

Utilizing hull space, meeting labor requirements, prioritizing perishable cargoes, tracking each shipping container as it moves about sea and land—all these tasks are computer-coordinated today. Gone are the days of the mate leaning over the bridge with a clipboard, counting individual barrels of olives going into the hold.

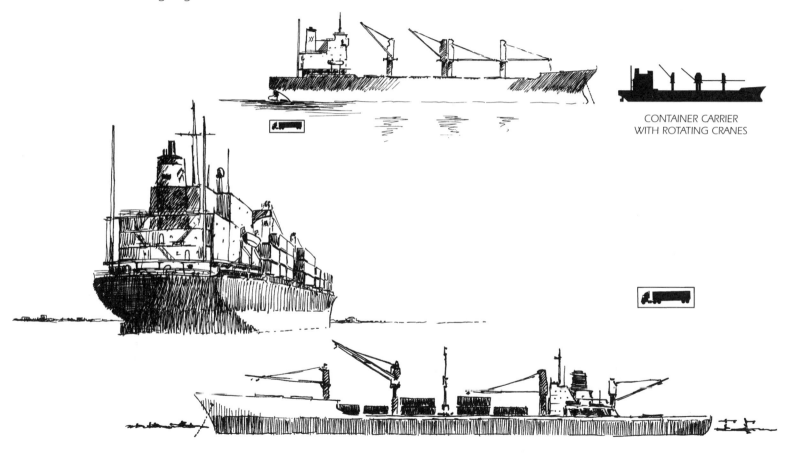

CONTAINER CARRIER
WITH ROTATING CRANES

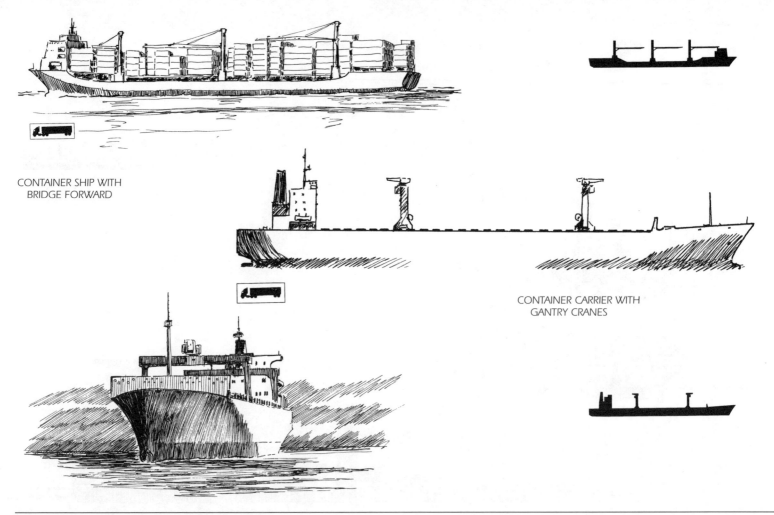

CONTAINER SHIP WITH
BRIDGE FORWARD

CONTAINER CARRIER WITH
GANTRY CRANES

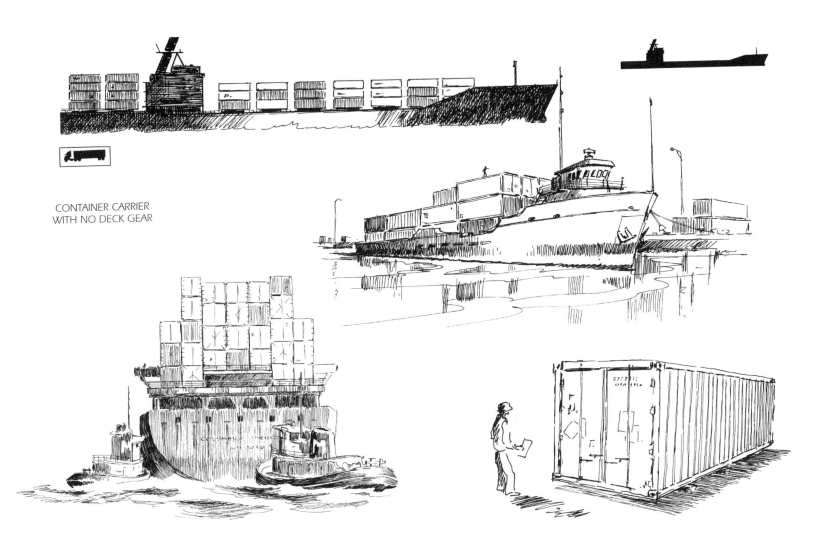

CONTAINER CARRIER
WITH NO DECK GEAR

NEO-BULK CARRIER

The neo-bulk ship is a multipurpose vessel designed to be flexible in cargo arrangements and competitive in a variety of trades; this to avoid layup time should a specific industry be undergoing its own economic recession.

At sea with a deckload of containers, a neo-bulk ship might appear to be a pure container carrier. Below, however, her holds may be configured to carry bulk cargoes of cement or grain, vehicles, bagged or barreled products on pallets, or any combination thereof.

The vessel may be fitted throughout the length of her cargo spaces with self-trimming holds for grain, or she may have a centerline bulkhead with each side of the hold serviced by its own hatch. Twin hatches and a centerline bulkhead allow for uneven loading times—one cargo is not dependent upon the other as to when it goes below. All neo-bulk carriers have hatches sized to carry a deckload of shipping containers.

Rotating cranes have eliminated the colorful jungle of rigging once required for masts and king posts, and can be put into service far more quickly.

VEHICLE CARRIER

The vehicle carrier is a specialized variation of the roll-on/roll-off ship. Due to her predictable cargo (this year's model), her space is configured to carry the maximum number of new trucks and automobiles from the manufacturer to international markets. A vehicle carrier can transport more than 4,000 vehicles at a time.

Look for high sides; ramps forward, aft, and in the sides; and ventilators, which are necessary to vent exhaust fumes while automobiles are loaded and unloaded under their own power.

INTEGRATED BARGE and TUG

She may look like a single vessel, but this is a 150-foot tug with her bow pinned into a recess in the stern of a 568-foot roll-on/roll-off barge. The tug is powered by twin diesels and can accommodate fourteen crew members. The barge can load approximately 144 standard 40-foot shipping containers by way of her bow ramp.

Traditionally, barges have been moved in open water with a tug either towing from ahead at the end of a long hawser, or positioned alongside with the tug's stern extending aft of the barge's stern. Towing with a long hawser reduces the chance of damage from contact between the two hulls in heavy seas. But there are dangerous disadvantages to towing a barge, especially at night. If the crew is late in detecting erratic behavior from the barge, such as not following the tug's course changes and continuing happily on her original course—or even sinking—the tug is in for trouble. The tug positioned alongside has better steering control and a quicker response time when changing course.

With the integrated barge and tug, the two hulls function as a single ship, minimizing hazards and reducing crew involvement during the tug's engagements and disengagements with the barge. The tug has only to snug into the recess in the barge's stern to activate two locking pins, one on each side of the tug, that slide into sockets in the inside shells of the recess.

From a distance the silhouette of the two hulls appears as one ship. Even from a closer vantage point, if the tug and barge have similar colors and company markings you may mistake the two for one. Since the beam of the tug is less by far than the beam of the barge, you may note irregular shadows and shades where the two hulls join.

There is a second method of engagement: The tug may embrace the barge with two "arms" around the outside of the barge shell. In this design, the tug is almost flush with the barge, and the presence of two hulls is even less noticeable.

BARGE CARRIER (LASH)

The major difference between the LASH (Lighters Aboard Ship) barge carrier and the SEABEE barge carrier (see page 106) is the method of stowing the barges. The SEABEE lifts the barge from the water to the desired deck level, then moves it into the hull through the ship's transom. The LASH barge carrier lifts the barge with a gantry—using cables attached to quick-connect fittings on the four corners of the barge—and moves the barge forward along the weather deck to be lowered through a hatch opening into the desired hold. The LASH carrier can hold only one standard-size barge.

HEAVY-LIFT CARGO SHIP

Should you need a pair of diesel locomotives delivered to the mouth of the Amazon, this may be the ship for you. Heavy-lift ships are built with long, undivided holds to accept massive loads of unpredictable lengths and shapes. They carry their own heavy-lift booms to do the job. Some have list-sensing devices that automatically transfer the water ballast to the high side of the ship, compensating for unacceptable heeling angles induced by a heavy load suspended over one side. Life aboard is never as routine on a heavy-lift ship as on a container ship, because each new cargo presents a new loading, stowage, and delivery challenge.

A variation of the heavy-lift ship type is a roll-on/roll-off vessel with loading ramps forward and aft; these allow heavy loads to be delivered by vehicle directly to the weather deck. This ship has oversized ballast tanks at both ends to correct for unacceptable changes in longitudinal trim (settling at the bow or stern) when the ramps are being used for loading.

Heavy-lift vessels are generally in the range of 300 feet long, and are diesel-powered. A roll-on/roll-off heavy-lift is distinguishable by the asymmetrical arrangement of her large king posts and lifting gear, which are located well outboard of her centerline, toward the port side.

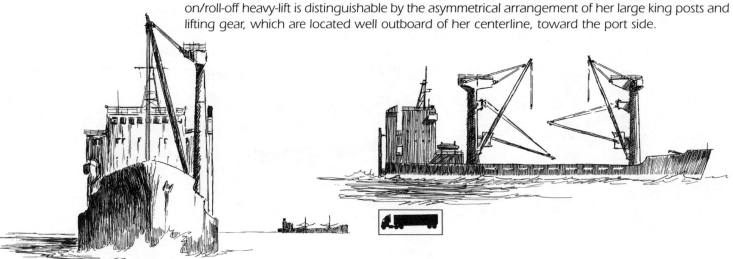

FLOAT-ON/FLOAT-OFF SHIP

The FO/FO could be defined as a self-propelled dry dock; both work on the same principle. The ballast tanks are flooded with seawater until the deck submerges to a depth sufficient to allow ungainly floating cargoes—such as prefabricated ship sections, offshore drilling rigs, or barge cranes—to be loaded on deck. With the vessel positioned over prepared keel blocks on the FO/FO's deck, water is pumped from the flooded tanks; as the ship rises, she lifts the load along with her. A bit of work with tie-downs and all is done. In this way, small vessels and structures unable to make long voyages under their own power, or too awkward in form or stability to be towed, can be transported any place in the world and floated off. Float-on/float-off ships are often converted tankers.

WHAT SHIP IS THAT?

PASSENGER and VEHICLE FERRY

With high, vertical sides that reveal no interruption between the hull and superstructure, and with a company name in large, smartly styled letters covering a goodly portion of her side, the deep-sea passenger ferry may resemble a carrier of the type used for delivering new automobiles. However, the ferry's vehicle doors and ramps are less conspicuous, and when closed, they fair into the hull with no exposed hinge assemblies or handling gear. A boat deck with a row of lifeboats indicates a large passenger-carrying capacity.

Given a choice between traveling by airplane or by ferry, take the ferry. I once crossed the Irish Sea from Holyhead to Dún Laoghaire in November on a *Sealink* ferry, with the wind gusting to Force 9 (47 to 54 mph) from the northwest and kicking up a nasty sea. A memorable passage. Considering the vessel's barnlike sides, she was amazingly stable—although not stable enough for all of the passengers that day. There was little action in the "casino" room, and even less in the bar. The dining room staff had posted a tempting lunch, but had few takers. Most folks sat expressionless, like commuters on the train from Grand Central to White Plains—all except a party of three couples snugged into a cozy nook of a lee weather deck. They were bundled together under deck blankets, wearing tam-o'-shanters and drinking Guinness stout. When they started singing I was convinced they were performers hired by the ship to provide ambience and entertainment for the passengers. They were amazed that I thought them actors. It seems they made the passage about once a week and had learned to take advantage of a welcome interruption in the otherwise fast pace of their trip.

WHAT SHIP IS THAT?

CRUISE LINER

Everyone not alert enough to tune out TV commercials must recognize the cruise liner. Gleaming white, her deck lined with lifeboats, her sides pierced with as many portholes as space will permit—to allow a "view of the sea" for all who can afford an outside cabin—the cruise liner would be hard to mistake for anything else. Besides, they all seem to have names containing words like Island, Princess, Fiesta, or Holiday. You can rearrange those words and produce all sorts of good names for cruise liners: Island Fiesta, Princess Island, Island Holiday. It's an adman's dream.

I must admit I've never sailed aboard one. I have trouble with the idea of sailing about with nothing to do—no lines to pull, passageways marked FOR CREW ONLY. I suspect the owners wouldn't let me steer the vessel, take sun sights and plot a position, or even muck about at odd hours in the machinery spaces. And how would I deal with traveling around without being bothered by border guards, visas, passports, customs agents, or currency rates? However, if the healthy-looking people sitting around the pool and the smart-dressed crowd at the elaborate buffet are enjoying themselves as much as the brochure photos imply, maybe I could go for it after all.

REMOVING A SPOT OF MUD FROM THE ANCHOR
ON THE *SKY PRINCESS*

MILITARY AND GOVERNMENT VESSELS

NAVY

BALLISTIC-MISSILE SUBMARINE, SSBN

A ballistic-missile submarine is the nation's most formidable and elusive defense system—a silent, nearly undetectable launching platform for Trident missiles. Perhaps never before has humanity utilized existing technology so successfully to design and build not just a defensive weapon, but also a deterrent against even being attacked.

Nuclear-powered submarines are so "slick" that they have few outstanding features to aid identification. Submarines can present numerous profiles, with none providing positive ID. A ballistic-missile sub is 200 feet longer than an attack submarine, but knowing this will do you little good unless you see the two together. The amount of hull showing above the water can vary considerably in height and length, depending upon the amount of water ballast aboard and upon the trim. You can often find the aft end of the boat by the tip of the rudder, which appears to be traveling independently in the wake, but you can never say with certainty where the bow begins. The sail is the sub's predominant feature, but at a distance all sails look pretty much alike. A ballistic-missile sub has a bit of a break aft in the flat of the deck, where it fairs into the round hull, which isn't present on the continuously round "turtle back" of an attack submarine.

You're unlikely to see a submarine traveling at high speed on the surface, leaving a wake as wide as a four-lane interstate highway and making that impressive bow-wave. Such is the stuff of promotional photographs. All that foam represents a waste of energy. A sub is an underwater animal.

A word of caution before you announce to all on the boardwalk that you've spotted a sub "right over there!": Make sure she isn't a loaded oil barge with a small tug on her far side.

SSBN, Ohio class

Power: One nuclear reactor, two geared turbines, one shaft
Length: 560 feet
Crew: 15 officers, 140 enlisted
Speed: In excess of 23 mph

WHAT SHIP IS THAT?

ATTACK SUBMARINE, SSN

The attack submarine is designed to hunt and destroy enemy submarines and surface ships, with a secondary mission of intelligence-collecting. The most impressive design feature of the interior of any submarine is the total utilization of space. Not a cubic foot is without its purpose. You may spot a seemingly empty area under a walkway grating, or high in the overhead, but be assured it's there by design—to provide access to some piece of equipment.

Unlike the case of modern surface ships, the evolutionary line from the sailing navy to the submarine is hard to trace. But there is a connection, and it lies in the personnel and the jobs they perform. They're out there alone, connected to their government only by an ethereal thread of infrequent radio communications. When Admiral Nelson sailed the HMS *Victory* out of the Channel he was alone, England's lone and powerful representative, connected to his government only by dispatch ships that took a month or more to exchange vital information. Every change in wind or weather, every sighting of a sail or flag influenced the way Nelson could fulfill his mission. There could be no consulting with his superiors at home. This is much the same sort of responsibility carried by the crew of a departing submarine when she slips quietly beneath the surface just before sunrise.

I think what intrigues any boat-watcher about subs is the incongruity of an unassuming, simple, dark form moving silently—but concealing a tightly controlled destructive potential. But keep it in perspective: A sub you spot these days is most likely moving upriver to be dry-docked for a bit of painting.

SSN, Los Angeles class

Power: One nuclear reactor, two geared turbines, one shaft
Length: 360 feet
Crew: 13 officers, 120 enlisted
Speed: In excess of 23 mph

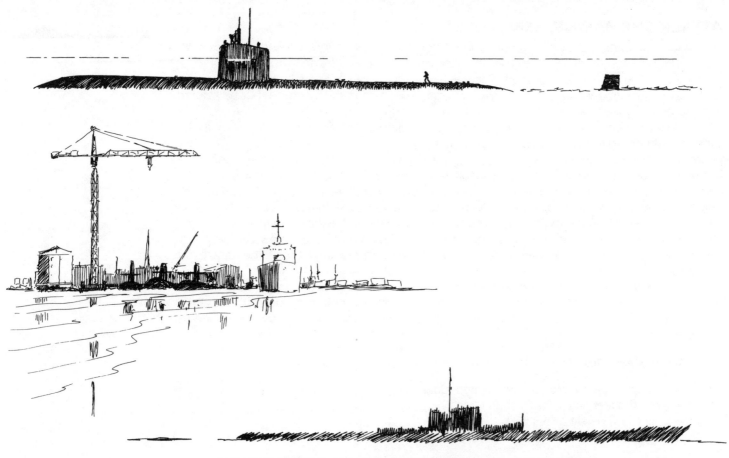

THIS LOOKS LIKE A SUB, BUT IT'S A BARGE WITH A SMALL TUG ON THE FAR SIDE.

AIRCRAFT CARRIER, CVN and CV

The carrier is the major player in the U.S. Navy's strategy for maintaining unrestricted use of the world's oceans. Deployable worldwide, wherever an airport is needed, the carrier has replaced the battleship as the premier platform for showing the flag.

Largest of all naval vessels, with well over 5,000 crew members and air-wing personnel, a carrier is indeed a self-contained city, with her own closed-circuit television, bakeries, medical and dental centers, barbershops, laundries, machine shops, aircraft repair and maintenance facilities, weapons magazines, meteorological station, electronics shops, fire and police forces, fleet of small boats—even ice cream–making equipment.

Visitors to a carrier will find the flight deck a place unlike any other—a combination of airfield, blacktopped parking lot, sports stadium, and rooftop. At first the atmosphere seems casual, almost parklike—crew members relaxing and soaking up the sun, joggers with sweatbands and hundred-yard stares, perhaps small family groups being escorted by proud crew members. But when you look closer you'll notice that large chunks of the deck are in fact enormous aircraft or weapons elevators. You'll see the four aircraft-launching catapults, and the thick wire cables stretched athwartships to catch the tailhooks of returning aircraft. In minutes this place can change from promenade deck to one of the most dangerous workplaces in the world. Here, man and metal operate at the edge of performance in an environment of screaming noises, swirling catapult steam, shooting sparks, smoking oil, and whipping cables.

At first you may mistake a carrier for an amphibious assault ship, which has a similar profile: a flat deck with a single, offset island house. If in doubt, count the openings in the sides; these accommodate the aircraft elevators that move planes from the hangar deck to the flight deck. A carrier has three openings on the starboard side, and one on the port. The opening on the port side is directly opposite the last opening on the starboard side, and if the doors are open you can see a bit of sky through the hangar deck. There's no such configuration on an amphibious assault ship.

CVN, Nimitz class

Power: Two nuclear reactors, four geared steam turbines, four shafts
Length: 1,040 feet
Ship's crew: 160 officers, 2,900 enlisted
Air-wing personnel: 190 officers, 1,915 enlisted
Speed: In excess of 34.5 mph

CVN, Enterprise class

Power: Eight nuclear reactors, four geared steam turbines, four shafts
Length: 1,040 feet
Ship's crew: 170 officers, 2,950 enlisted
Air-wing personnel: 230 officers, 1,800 enlisted
Speed: In excess of 34.5 mph

CV, John F. Kennedy class

Power: Eight boilers, four geared steam turbines, four shafts
Length: 1,052 feet
Ship's crew: 135 officers, 2,440 enlisted
Air-wing personnel: 220 officers, 1,305 enlisted
Speed: In excess of 34.5 mph

PORT SIDE

WHAT SHIP IS THAT?

CV, Kitty Hawk class

Power: Eight boilers, four geared steam turbines, four shafts
Length: 1,062 feet
Ship's crew: 125 officers, 2,400 enlisted
Air-wing personnel: 200 officers, 1,230 enlisted
Speed: In excess of 34.5 mph

CV, Forrestal class

Power: Eight boilers, four geared steam turbines, four shafts
Length: 1,063 feet
Ship's crew: 125 officers, 2,260 enlisted
Air-wing personnel: 170 officers, 1,425 enlisted
Speed: In excess of 34.5 mph

 STARBOARD SIDE

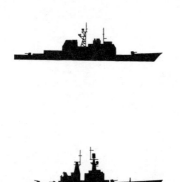

GUIDED-MISSILE CRUISER, CG (non-nuclear) and CGN (nuclear)

Since the retirement of the battleship, the guided-missile cruiser has moved to the top of the line of surface-combat vessels. The cruiser is capable of operating independently, or in concert with carrier battle groups, or as a flagship for lesser combat vessels grouped for specific action.

Today's cruiser carries no big guns like the battleship's—only two 5-inch guns and two 20mm Phalanx close-in weapons systems. The cruiser's threat to the enemy is stowed below—guided missiles. The objects on her fore and aft decks, generally assumed to be missiles by visitors to naval ports, are most likely only missile launchers.

The most readily identifiable features of the *Ticonderoga* class (CG) are the barnlike ends of her superstructure and the stacks of her conventional power plants. On the nuclear-powered vessels of the *Virginia* class(CGN), look for the unbroken line of the sheer and the gap in the middle of the housing.

CG, Ticonderoga class

Power: Four gas turbines, two shafts
Length: 567 feet
Crew: 24 officers, 340 enlisted
Speed: In excess of 34.5 mph

CGN, Virginia class

Power: Two nuclear reactors, two geared turbines, two shafts
Length: 585 feet
Crew: 39 officers, 539 enlisted
Speed: 34.5 mph

CG

CG

CGN

GUIDED-MISSILE DESTROYER, DDG

Guided-missile destroyers are warships assigned to protect carrier and amphibious battle groups. Fast, and armed to the teeth with antiair and antisurface missiles, they exist to provide early detection and immediate response to the enemy. An oversimplified definition of their mission is to "slug it out" while the special-mission ships of the force get on with their jobs.

When the class was initiated in 1991 with the commissioning of the *Arleigh Burke*, the guided-missile destroyer was probably more formidable than any previous surface ship in history.

DDG, Arleigh Burke class

Power: Four gas turbines, two shafts
Length: 466 feet
Crew: 23 officers, 300 enlisted
Speed: 35.7 mph

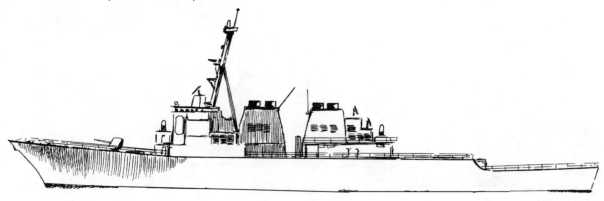

WHAT SHIP IS THAT?

DESTROYER, DD

Along with the submarine, the destroyer has been the vessel most often selected for sea stories and motion pictures. As a result, she's the ship we all feel we know, the ship of *The Caine Mutiny,* of *The Enemy Below,* and of the greatest destroyer tale of them all: Marcus Goodrich's *Delilah,* the story of a pre–World War I four-stacker.

The destroyer's primary purpose remains antisubmarine warfare. She, along with the frigate, could be considered the light cavalry of the service. Or maybe the sheepdog, constantly circling the perimeter of her flock.

DD, Spruance class

Power: Four gas turbines, two shafts
Length: 563 feet
Crew: 30 officers, 352 enlisted
Speed: 38 mph

WHAT SHIP IS THAT?

GUIDED-MISSILE FRIGATE, FFG

Her movements in and out of a port attract little attention from waterfront regulars. Generally assigned to escort replenishment ships and merchant convoys against air and submarine attack, the frigate lacks the capability to resist modern high-tech weapons. With limited capacity for upgrading programs, the frigate's future is uncertain. Despite these limitations, two frigates that received crippling damage in recent wars survived to sail again with the fleet; one ship struck a mine, and the other received two hits from Exocet missiles.

Should one come your way, I suggest you give her a bit of attention. There are a lot of railroad buffs around today who regret not having paid a little more attention to the steam locomotive back in the 1950s.

FFG, Oliver Hazard Perry class

Power: Two gas turbines, one shaft
Length: 445 feet
Crew: 13 officers, 287 enlisted
Speed: 33.4 mph

AMPHIBIOUS ASSAULT SHIP, LHD, LHA, and LPH

There's little of the graceful or aesthetic about an amphibious assault ship. Designed to put men, weapons, vehicles, and supplies ashore under hostile conditions, amphibious assault ships are virtual floating marine camps, with all the facilities you'd expect. They are vast honeycombs of stowage spaces, rapid cargo-handling conveyors and elevators, weapons magazines, vehicle garages, and hospital, berthing, and messing spaces for combat troops. Their sole purpose is to establish marines in secure positions on shores where other people don't want them to be.

Regardless of their aircraft-carrier appearance, amphibious ships are not rigged to launch and recover fixed-wing fighters; their flight decks are for helicopters that convey marines and combat supplies ashore. However, the decks can also accommodate Harrier vertical-takeoff fighter-bombers and antisubmarine helicopters.

The LHD and the LHA also perform beach assaults with conventional and air-cushion landing craft, launched through stern gates opening directly onto the sea.

Always in search of lingering customs from the sailing navy when aboard a naval ship, it was on an LHD that I witnessed a sailor sentenced to confinement on bread and water. Tried on the main deck before the captain, with the ship's company in attendance, he was sentenced and quick-marched away. Not as colorful a rite as it might have been on the *Bounty*—no backing of the main yards during the proceedings, no snare drums, no bosun calls—but pretty much the same to the chap in the brig.

LHD, Wasp class

Power: Two boilers, two geared turbines, two shafts
Length: 844 feet
Ship's crew: 104 officers, 1,004 enlisted
Marine detachment: 1,894
Speed: 23 mph

LHA, Tarawa class

Power: Two boilers, two geared turbines, two shafts
Length: 833 feet
Ship's crew: 58 officers, 882 enlisted
Marine detachment: 1,900
Speed: 27.5 mph

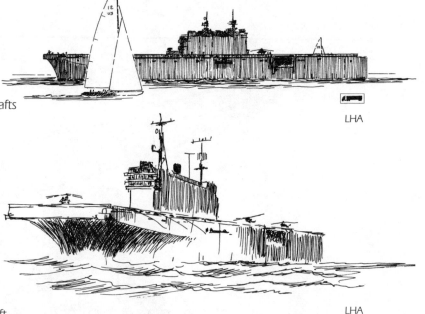

LHA

LHA

LPH, Iwo Jima class

Power: Two boilers, one geared turbine, one shaft
Length: 602 feet
Ship's crew: 47 officers, 638 enlisted
Marine detachment: 2,000
Speed: 26.5 mph

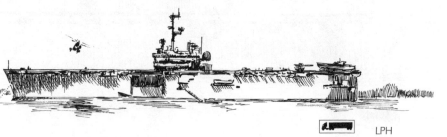

LPH

DOCK LANDING SHIP, LSD

It seems that the more recent the design, the more ungainly and unattractive a vessel becomes. With her "warehouse" superstructure perched well forward, you may mistake the LSD for one of the large roll-on/roll-off cargo ships. But this is a fighting ship, designed to assault contested shores. The LSD is built specifically to accommodate four air-cushion landing craft and provide docking and repair facilities for both air-cushion craft and conventional landing craft.

LSD, Whidbey Island class

Power: Four 16-cylinder diesels, two shafts
Length: 609 feet
Ship's crew: 22 officers, 391 enlisted
Marine detachment: 400 to 500
Speed: 23 mph

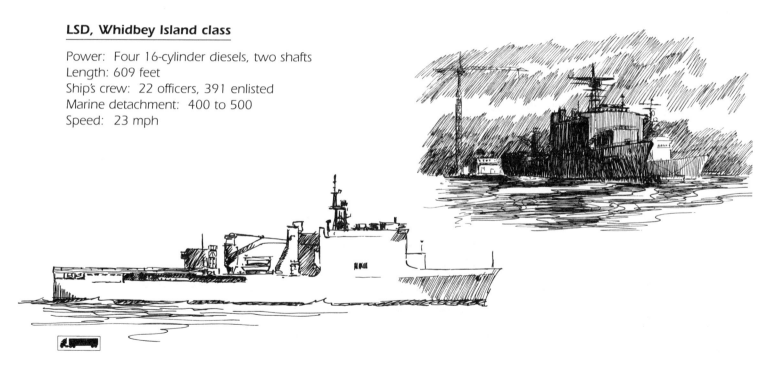

AMPHIBIOUS TRANSPORT, DOCK, LPD

The Austin-class LPDs, built between 1965 and 1971, have a bit of age on them now, but they're still up to the mark for troop transportation and participation in amphibious operations. From a well-deck opening to the sea through the stern, the ship can debark troops and their gear via landing craft or amphibious vehicles, and via helicopter from a large flight deck aft. The transport's profile may change with the deployment of her helicopter hangar, which can be collapsed or extended somewhat like a telescope.

LPD, Austin class

Power: Two boilers, two steam turbines, two shafts
Length: 570 feet
Ship's crew: 24 officers, 396 enlisted
Marine detachment: 900
Speed: 24 mph

AMPHIBIOUS CARGO SHIP, LKA

From a distance, you may mistake the amphibious cargo ship for an old merchant freighter. She was, in fact, one of the very first naval vessels specifically designed to carry heavy equipment and supplies to support troop landings. Large landing craft and heavy-lift rigging are distinctive features that will aid your identification. These ships move in and out of the reserve fleet with some regularity, depending on the pressing needs of the government.

LKA, Charleston class

Power: Two boilers, one steam turbine, one shaft
Length: 575 feet
Ship's crew: 30 officers, 357 enlisted
Troops: 226
Speed: 23 mph

DESTROYER TENDER, AD

The official purpose of a destroyer tender is to repair battle damage to destroyers. In fact, destroyer tenders are capable of repairing and providing maintenance for most any type of naval vessel, including nuclear-powered ships during wartime conditions. Their normal station is at anchor in a protected harbor or at pierside, with the ship requiring their services moored nearby or alongside. A larger percentage of crew members are ship-repair specialists and technicians with expertise in electronics and weapons. They are almost, as they brag, capable of cloning their own vessel. I lived aboard a tender in a Mediterranean port for a week installing a huge roll-up door on the helicopter hangar. The crew provided all of the labor, skills, and equipment I needed to accomplish the job, which consisted of burning holes in steel plates and extensive welding, plus repairing a pair of eyeglasses I dropped down a ladder well. Clever fellows.

There's little of the graceful about these ships; they're getting on in years and have been worked hard. Their clearest identifying features are the two 30-ton cranes located about a third of the ship's length from the stern.

AD, Yellowstone and Gompers class

Power: Two boilers, steam turbines, one shaft
Length: 645 feet
Crew: 42 officers, 1,380 enlisted
Speed: 23 mph

AMMUNITION SHIP, AE

Looking nondescript and much like a general cargo freighter, the ammunition ship has the unenviable task of delivering munitions to warships on station. She's capable of transferring ammunition and ordnance by slings on ship-to-ship cables, or by helicopter. You may see a CH-46 Sea Knight helicopter on her landing deck.

AE, Kilauea class

Power: Three boilers, steam turbines, one shaft
Length: 564 feet
Crew: 17 officers, 366 enlisted
Speed: 23 mph

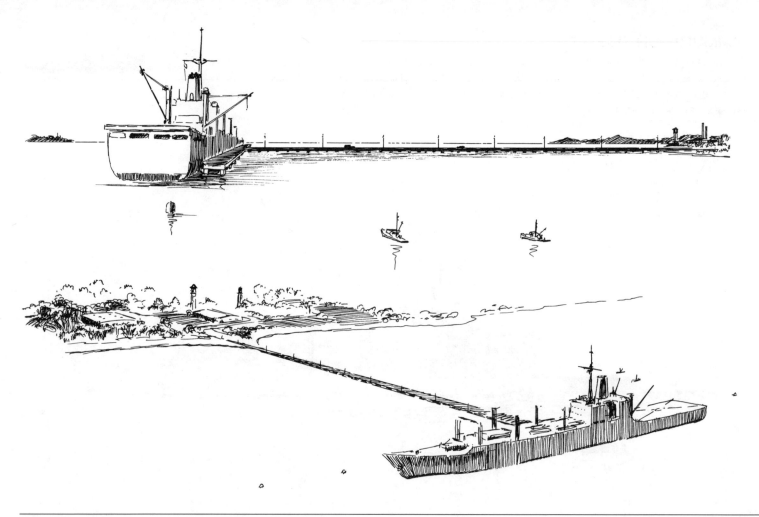

WHAT SHIP IS THAT?

FLEET OILER, AO

The fleet oiler is the military version of a merchant tanker, transporting bulk petroleum to naval stations and bases throughout the world. Oiler numbers are decreasing as the job becomes increasingly entrusted to Military Sealift Command ships with civilian crews. An AO can carry 180,000 barrels of fuel. The long openings in the sides are identifying features.

AO, Cimarron class

Power: Two boilers, one steam turbine, one shaft
Length: 708 feet
Crew: 15 officers, 318 enlisted
Speed: 23 mph

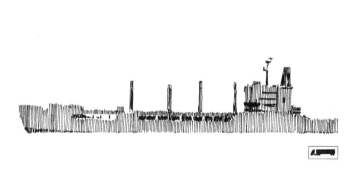

FAST COMBAT-SUPPORT SHIP, AOE

Many duties, capabilities, and mission purposes overlap among the fast combat-support ship, the replenishment oiler and the fleet oiler. All can be defined as supply ships, with a primary function of delivering fuel oil, petroleum products, ammunition, and dry stores to ships underway or on station. The AOE is the largest of the three, with the ability to carry 177,000 barrels of oil, 2,150 tons of ammunition, 500 tons of dry stores, and 250 tons of refrigerated stores—and the speed required to keep up with a carrier battle group.

Refueling at sea, even under ideal conditions, is hazardous. The supply vessel and the receiving ship often close to within 100 feet or less while maintaining parallel courses and identical speeds. An automatic tensioning device, sensitive to changes induced by the motion of the sea, continually adjusts the tension on the span wire to keep it constant, but can compensate for only limited changes in ship positions. The crew members on the bridges of both ships must never lose their concentration on maintaining speed and course. A momentary lapse could result in a collision, or a messy parting of the cables and hose.

The refueling procedure is a step-by-step, "by-the-book" operation that establishes a span wire between the ships on which to suspend the refueling hose. The procedure and rigging will vary among ship types due to variations in hose size and to the customized use of fairlead blocks and winches. The drill consists of much passing of lines: first the telephone cable, then messenger lines, and then retrieving lines; finally, the hose is sent across suspended from "saddles" riding on the span wire.

The plan is for the vessel requiring fuel to make an approach and come abeam of the oiler, then rig the hose, transfer the fuel, break down the rig, send the components back to the responsible ship, and move on quickly. Performing at high speeds is not macho show-off; reducing the time that the two vessels are connected also reduces the vulnerability of both oiler and customer to the enemy.

The last line released and sent back to the vessel being supplied is the communications cable. Crew members from the supplying ship, which has such luxuries as a full-service bakery, often attach a waterproof bag filled with donuts and cookies.

   Outstanding features of the AOE are king posts with fixed booms (or outriggers), cantilevered outboard. You'll be able to see the hose hanging in loops from the peak of the outrigger down to the deck. The bulk of her housing is forward, with a lower structure aft with the stack.

AOE, Sacramento class

Power: Four boilers, geared turbines, two shafts
Length: 793 feet
Crew: 24 officers, 576 enlisted
Speed: 30 mph

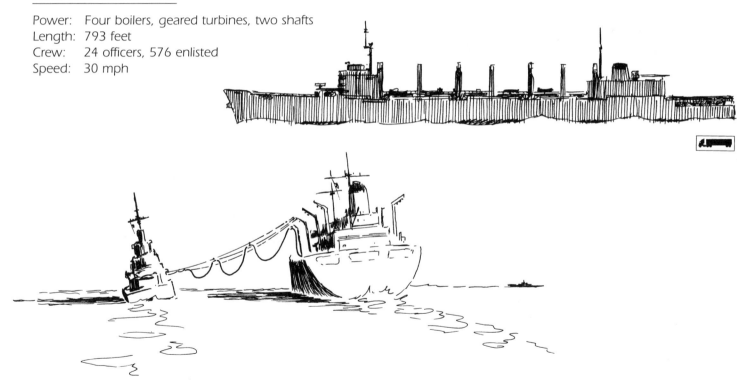

REPLENISHMENT OILER, AOR

Smaller than a fast combat-support ship, the replenishment oiler is also capable of supplying carrier battle groups with petroleum and munitions. Even at close range, you may have some trouble distinguishing her from a fleet oiler (AO); both have a large superstructure aft, but the AOR has a bridge deck forward.

The AOR carries 160,000 barrels of petroleum, 600 tons of munitions, 200 tons of dry stores, and 100 tons of refrigerated stores.

AOR, Wichita class

Power: Three boilers, steam turbines, two shafts
Length: 659 feet
Crew: 24 officers, 448 enlisted
Speed: 23 mph

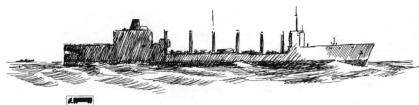

HARBOR TUG, YTB

Other than being painted gray and black and having "YTB" painted on her bow, there is little to distinguish a navy tug from any other large harbor tug. Her daily work is pushing about navy barges and nudging ships into naval dry docks for overhaul. The skipper is usually a petty officer. Considering the hourly rate a commercial tug charges, the taxpayer is getting a bargain from the YTB.

This is the craft you'll see spraying colored water from its fire-fighting apparatus atop the pilothouse when a carrier and its escorts are returning from a lengthy deployment at sea. The performance is all pomp and show, abandoned in a moment if a crosscurrent or fluky wind begins to set the carrier out of the channel. The YTB's real purposes are to prevent grounding and to help execute a successful docking. Everyone gets a bit edgy when a carrier enters confined spaces. You may notice the tug's presence in the mouth of the harbor, indifferently lounging in the morning mist an hour before the inbound ships ever appear on the horizon.

YTB tug

Power: Diesel
Length: 108 feet
Crew: 8 to 12
Speed: 13 mph

YRBM

BERTHING BARGE, YRBM and APL

I don't know if berthing barges have skippers or not. If so, their workplace is a long way from a destroyer's bridge. Berthing barges are as likely to be moored at a private contractor's yard as in a naval facility, for they're used to house crew members displaced from their ships during overhaul or repair, and to provide offices and workshops for crew members with special expertise needed temporarily at a particular location. With air-conditioned messing and berthing spaces, they're about as nice as an inexpensive motel.

Seen from the river against an industrial background, a berthing barge may appear to be a gray warehouse. Look for the television antennas and the rat guards. A word about rats: They've been aboard ships ever since the first vessel ran up a flag and called itself a navy. In the sailing navy there was a balance among the ship's cats, the traps, the food available, and the rats. Still, the balance was more favorable to the rats than the crew. "Rats deserting a sinking ship" has real meaning. It's the rat that first comes into contact with unwanted seawater inside a ship, and therefore it's the rat that's the first to scurry for higher places.

The last 200 years have seen leaps and bounds in the evolution of ships. A sailor from the Continental Navy would stand in uncomprehending awe of a nuclear-powered cruiser, and an aircraft carrier would boggle his mind. However, I suspect that should a present-day ship's rat meet one of his own kind from the *Bonhomme Richard,* they would become immediate comrades with the same seagoing savvy and problems.

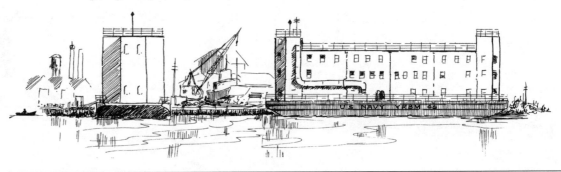

"I HEAR SHE'S BOUND FOR SINGAPORE;
I HAVE A COUSIN THERE."

APL

TANK LANDING SHIP, LST

The tank landing ship, made conspicuous by the two "horns" protruding over her bow, is designed to deliver land tanks ashore in an amphibious assault. The horns are used in the deployment of a 112-foot ramp over the bow to off-load vehicles and cargo. The "ramp-over-the-bow" design allows the hull shape necessary to reach the speeds required to sail with a modern assault force. The old World War II drop-down bow ramp, though simpler in operation, precluded the higher speeds needed for modern military missions.

LST, Newport class

Power: Six diesels, two shafts
Length: 522 feet
Crew: 13 officers, 244 enlisted
Speed: 23 mph

BATTLESHIP, BB

The last four battleships of the U.S. Navy—BB 61 *Iowa*, BB 62 *New Jersey*, BB 63 *Missouri*, and BB 64 *Wisconsin*—are all presently decommissioned and awaiting decisions as to their final disposition. Being permanently moored as a tourist attraction in a waterfront park is about the best that could be expected; the worst, being towed to the breaker's yard for scrap. Not an easy choice for those in charge of old battleships, but there are some guidelines. Old ships have been sunk, burnt, or broken up for scrap since the beginning of navies; it's only recently that they've been plugged into dockside utility systems, not unlike life-support tubes, and had their usefulness extended as restaurants and gift shops.

The *Iowa* carried President Franklin D. Roosevelt to Casablanca, on the first leg of his journey to Tehran for a conference with Churchill and Stalin; the *Missouri* provided a stage for the official end to World War II. All fought in the Pacific war. The *Iowa* was the first-built of these four ships; she was launched in August of 1942, followed by the *New Jersey* in December of 1942, the *Wisconsin* in December of 1943, and the *Missouri* in January of 1944.

Time has rendered these mammoth warriors inadequate for modern naval strategy. Built to engage their worthy opponents one on one, slugging it out with 16-inch guns, or to soften the resistance to a beach landing by prolonged bombardment, they no longer have a job. Smaller and more economical vessels can achieve the same results. Battleships last saw action in the Gulf War, launching Tomahawk missiles against Iraqi-held targets and bombarding shore emplacements with the big guns.

Battleships are gigantic and gray, have big guns, are salty, can make smoke, are linked directly to the sailing navy's "ships of the line," and can impress the hell out of people when they appear from the morning fog. The battleship embodied national pride at its best. The stuff of empire, the stuff of history. If you see one being towed to her final resting place, feel fortunate.

BB, Iowa class

Power: Eight boilers, four GE turbines, two five-blade propellers, two four-blade propellers
Length: 887 feet, 3 inches
Beam: 108 feet, 3 inches
Draft: 38 feet
Height: From keel to mast top, 209 feet, 8 inches
Crew (World War II): 134 officers, 2,400 enlisted
Speed: In excess of 34.5 mph
Main Guns: Nine 16-inch guns in three turrets
Armor: 13$\frac{1}{2}$-inch-thick hull in vital locations

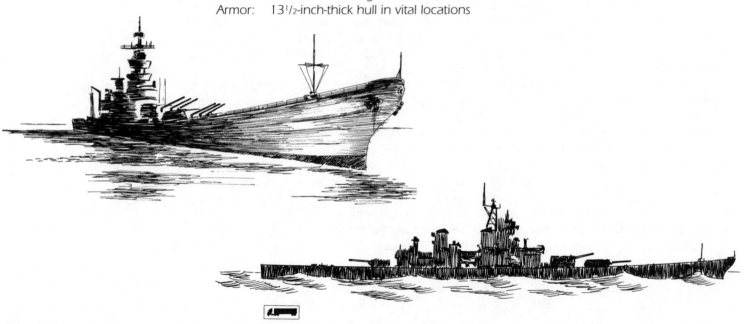

MILITARY SEALIFT COMMAND and the
READY RESERVE FORCE

Ready Reserve Force ships are maintained in a reduced operating status by the United States Maritime Administration in five-, ten-, or twenty-day categories of **readiness**—the time it would require to make them operational. The majority of the Ready Reserve ships are moored in the United States, distributed among Suisun Bay, California; Beaumont, Texas; and Hampton Roads, Virginia. Others of the fleets are pre-positioned around the world, loaded with military supplies and ready to be first on the scene of any global conflict. During the Persian Gulf War they delivered 95 percent of the cargo used.

The fleet consists of all types of cargo vessels, from a few very old break-bulk freighters to the new roll-on/roll-off ships. Most of these ships were originally engaged in commercial trades until market conditions or poor management made them unprofitable. They were then acquired by the government to assure the availability of sufficient vessels to meet national emergencies. The ships of the Ready Reserve Force are manned by civilian crews and are easily identifiable by the red, white, and blue horizontal bands on their stacks.

Military Sealift Command and Ready Reserve Force ships use the same identification letters as regular navy vessels, preceded by a **T.**

Ships of the Military Sealift Command are non-combatant and crewed by civilians. Ship types include transport vessels, oilers, supply ships, and tugs. Some are government owned, others are chartered from private shipping firms. MSC ships can be quickly identified by the horizontal bands of black, gray, blue, and gold on their stacks.

FLEET OILER, T-AO (MILITARY SEALIFT COMMAND)

The Henry J. Kaiser–class fleet oiler is only a few feet shorter in length than the Cimarron-class oiler, but it is diesel-powered, just as fast, and offers replenishment of refrigerated and dry stores to the fleet. Manned by both navy and civilian personnel, these vessels are increasingly assuming the duties and responsibilities of 100 percent navy-manned fleet oilers.

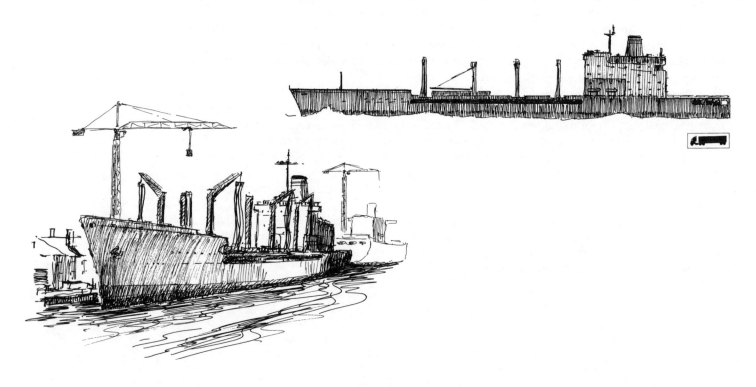

COMBAT-STORES SHIP, T-AFS (MSC)

Getting a bit old, and very much resembling a freighter from the 1960s and '70s, the Mars-class combat-stores ship performs freight-hauling duties for the navy. She's a fleet-support ship supplying general stores, spares, refrigerated and dry provisions, and mail. Cargo is discharged directly to ships tied alongside, or by helicopter. This ship is another workhorse.

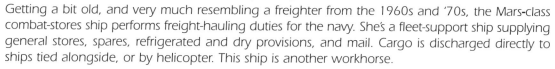

CABLE-REPAIR SHIP, T-ARC, SPECIAL MISSION-SUPPORT SHIP (MSC)

Built especially to lay and repair communications and data-transmitting cable at great depths, the *Zeus* is the only vessel with such abilities owned by the navy, and is crewed by civilian and naval personnel.

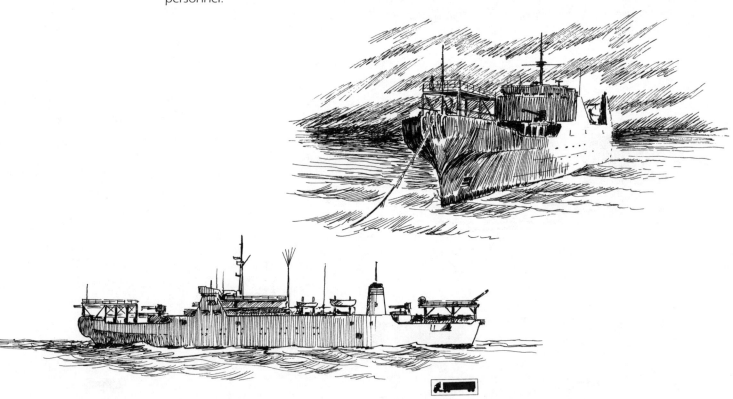

VEHICLE CARGO, T-AKR (MSC)

Classified as a Fast Sealift ship by the Military Sealift Command, and kept in a reserve category and crewed by civilians, the T-AKR can be operational in four days, making her capable of responding to the demands of a quick and massive buildup of military force anywhere in the world. Approaching the size and speed of aircraft carriers, eight of these vessels can transport the entire inventory of tanks, armored vehicles, trucks, and helicopters for a full army mechanized division.

These vessels were once commercial container ships; they were purchased by the U.S. government and modified with roll-on/roll-off ramps, additional lift capacity, and helicopter-landing platforms.

VEHICLE TRANSPORT, T-AKR (READY RESERVE FORCE)

This large roll-on/roll-off vessel, with her strange jumble of hinged ramps, platforms, crossovers, and lifting gear, could easily be mistaken by a sightseer for a factory building, especially if she's moored in the vicinity of industrial complexes such as chemical plants or oil refineries. The deck line is broken by regularly spaced ventilators, which are required for venting the exhaust fumes produced by drive-on vehicles.

C3 FREIGHTER, BREAK-BULK, T-AK (RRF)

Unprofitable in this age of container carriers, the old reliable break-bulk freighter still has a place in servicing undeveloped ports of the world where superterminals are unavailable, especially those requiring military supplies in irregular lots and sizes. With her own uncomplicated hatch covers and simple cargo-handling gear of masts, king posts, and booms, the traditional freighter is self-sufficient in discharging cargo. Using a 22-foot-diameter propeller, the ship has a design speed of 20 mph.

What appears to be the stack on this ship is shown on the 1959 general arrangement drawing as an emergency diesel generator room. The actual stacks, or uptakes, are just aft of the amidships superstructure and double as king posts with cargo booms. There was no real purpose in making the uppermost house resemble a stack; it just made the C3 look right and proper, and it now serves as a fine place for the red, white, and blue bands.

C5 FREIGHTER, BREAK-BULK, T-AK (RRF)

After World War II, freighters of this genre performed most of the world's shipping, filling the period between the Liberty and Victory Ships and today's giant container ships and bulk carriers. For most of the last sixty years, oil-fired cargo freighters—400 to 600 feet long, designed with a moderate sheer, rigged with their own cargo-handling gear of masts and booms, and crewed by men who chose the sea as a way of life and not because it offered overtime and a good dental plan—numbered in the thousands. Their demise at the hands of large-capacity, diesel-powered ships went unnoticed by the public, until only a few remained.

It seems that the last of any endangered species stays around disproportionately longer than the predecessors that disappeared early on, without fanfare. Examples: the MG-TD sports car, the DC-3 airplane—and the C5-type freighter. Enjoy them; they're pretty. By the way, the stack on this one is real, not just for show.

BARGE CARRIER, SEABEE, T-AKR (RRF)

The SEABEE barge carrier is chockablock full of massive, heavy, greasy, dangerous-to-be-around machinery—an engineering complexity of elevators, sheaves, pulleys, and cables; hydraulic winches, self-propelled barge transporters, electric position winches, tie-down and tensioning devices; power cables, limit switches, and control stations. The mechanics are complex but the concept is simple: Just bring the barge to the stern of the SEABEE, lift it from the water with an elevator, and send it forward for stowage on one of three decks. Total loading and unloading time, less than five days.

The SEABEE is ideally suited to ports fed by an inland waterway distribution system, as opposed to just railroads and highways. Showing two stacks, she's powered by one turbine and one shaft and propeller that can push her up to about 23 mph. She has facilities for a crew of forty-three.

SECTION CUT

SECTION

ROLL-ON/ROLL-OFF CARGO SHIP, T-AKR (RRF)

Awesome in size, ugly and poorly proportioned by classical standards, too expensive to operate commercially, the RO/RO is nevertheless perfectly suited for rapidly moving vast amounts of over-sized and odd-shaped military equipment. I once saw three of these ships moored side by side and bow to stern; they a baffling profilewas nearly impossible to sort out and identify until I viewed them ends-on. Look for the red, white, and blue bands on the two stacks. Further confusion in establishing identity may result from shipping containers stacked on her weather deck.

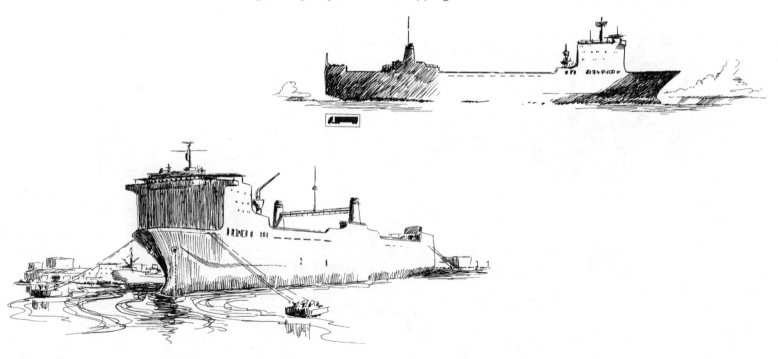

ARMY

LANDING CRAFT UTILITY, LCU 2000

The LCU has a range of 4,500 miles, making her capable of supplying troops anywhere in the world with containerized, break-bulk, and roll-on/roll-off cargo. Swift and maneuverable, she can be used for ferry service in congested harbors and inland waters. She has a speed of about 13 mph and a crew of twelve. The landing craft is powered by two turbocharged diesels, and is equipped with a stern anchor to aid in hauling herself away from a beach.

LOGISTIC SUPPORT VESSEL, LSV

This is the army's beach-landing ship for support of its own troops. Basically a drive-on/drive-off, cargo-landing barge, she can quickly load or discharge any vehicles required for supplying troops from the sea. She's 273 feet long; has a crew of twenty-nine, and a speed of 13 mph; and can deliver 2,000 tons of cargo. The vessel is equipped with a computer and communications system tied directly into the army's continental supply system, and can—from any location world-wide—determine the availability and source of spare parts, as well as maintenance procedures, for combat vehicles and equipment.

A thing to remember about large landing craft: If they appear to be "hard aground" on a hostile and contested beach, they may well be so. It's a bonus if a vessel can back off after delivering her supplies; a successful first landing is the primary mission.

LARGE OCEANGOING TUG, LT

The army's large tugs are much the same as any oceangoing tugs, except that they're fitted out for the army's special military needs. This type of tug is used for coastal and deep-sea towing, and for assisting large ships in docking. She has a cruising range (without barges) of more than 5,000 miles, and can maintain a speed of 5.75 mph when towing a maximum load of eight million pounds in five- to eight-foot seas.

Inside this seemingly ordinary tug are the following spaces and equipment: pilothouse, auxiliary control stations, damage control center, radio room, arms room, medical locker, electronics stores, life rafts, machine guns, workboat, boat-handling crane, anchor windlasses, the captain's and chief engineer's staterooms, crew's quarters, emergency generator room, bosun's locker, galley, freezer, dry stores locker, weather gear locker, recreation space, life jacket locker, laundry space, paint locker, towing winch, capstan, steering gear room, main and auxiliary machinery spaces, workshop, fuel and water tanks, lube-oil tanks, spare parts locker, bow thruster, and anchors and anchor chains. A lot of stuff!

COAST GUARD

BUOY-TENDER, COASTAL, WLM

The maintenance of sea buoys and lighthouses is the primary job of the coastal buoy-tender. It's a smelly business, hoisting aboard a sea buoy encrusted with barnacles, seaweed, kelp, and little marine creatures. Having silently performed its mission, the buoy is now covered with seabird droppings; its light has been reported as erratic; there's a dent in it from God knows what; and it must have taken in some water, for it seems to be floating 12 inches below its waterline.

Buoy-Tender, coastal, WLM

Power:	Two diesel engines
Length:	157 feet
Crew:	5 officers, 29 enlisted
Speed:	14.7 mph
Range:	4,500 miles

BUOY-TENDER, RIVER, WLR

You may mistake this tuglike buoy-tender, pushing her construction barge, for one long riverboat. Her job is to maintain day markers, can and nun buoys, and lighted beacons on lakes and inland waterways. The barge is equipped with a workshop and serves as a platform from which to drive pilings for the construction of new, or replacement, navigational aids. It goes without saying that all Coast Guard vessels, from a seagoing cutter to the most nondescript riverboat, will, in addition to their designed purposes, engage in search-and-rescue operations if so required.

The river buoy-tender, like her more glamorous sisters, is marked with the diagonal red band that says, in a very graphic fashion, COAST GUARD.

Buoy-Tender, river, WLR

Power: Two diesel engines
Length: 75 feet (tug)
Crew: 1 warrant officer, 13 enlisted
Range: 2,500 miles

This silhouette is typical of a Coast Guard cutter, but doesn't represent any one particular vessel. More important than silhouette in identifying Coast Guard vessels is the red diagonal stripe on the hull. It's found on all Coast Guard vessels and can be easily recognized at some distance, even in poor visibility.

ICEBREAKER, WAGB, 290-foot class

The mission of the Coast Guard icebreaker is to keep the shipping lanes of the Great Lakes and large rivers open and free of ice for merchant shipping. The outstanding feature of the icebreaker is the design of the bow, which allows the ship to ride onto the ice and then crush it with her own weight. Not surprisingly, the paint on the bow always seems to need a bit of touching up. Ice up to six feet thick can be broken and pushed aside at a speed of 3.75 mph—producing alarming sounds inside the hull. Icebreakers have reinforced hulls and a water ballast system that allows for quick changes in ship trim to increase their effectiveness at attacking and breaking ice.

WAGB, 290-foot class

Power: Six diesel engines
Length: 290 feet
Crew: 8 officers, 67 enlisted
Speed: 20.7 mph
Range: 41,000 miles at half speed

MEDIUM-ENDURANCE CUTTER, WMEC, 270-foot class

Search and rescue, coastal surveillance, and law enforcement are the basic missions of the medium-endurance cutter—the same as those of the high-endurance cutter, but slightly limited by the smaller ship's reduced speed and cruising range.

WMEC, 270-foot class

Power: Two diesel engines
Length: 270 feet
Crew: 13 officers, 96 enlisted
Speed: 22.4 mph
Range: 9,900 miles

HIGH-ENDURANCE CUTTER, WHEC, 378-foot class

By definition, a **cutter** is any Coast Guard vessel over 65 feet long with living accommodations for her crew. The high-endurance cutter is the largest of a fleet of cutters in service, and—as her name implies—she has the ability to stay on station in nasty weather for long periods of time. Primary missions: search and rescue, coastal surveillance, and law enforcement.

WHEC, 378-foot class

Power: Two diesel engines, or two gas turbines
Length: 378 feet
Crew: 16 officers, 162 enlisted
Speed: 33.4 mph
Range: 14,000 miles

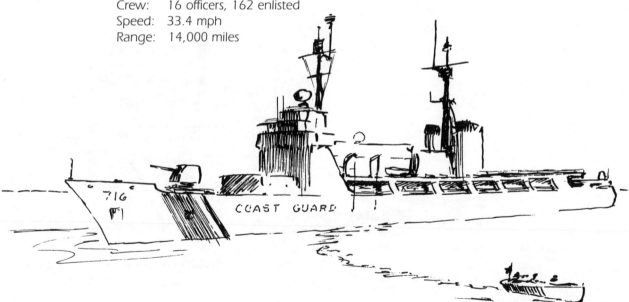

NATIONAL OCEANIC AND ATMOSPHERIC ADMINISTRATION (NOAA)

SURVEY VESSEL

There's a varied fleet of NOAA research and survey vessels, ranging in size from 90 feet—a ship that normally operates off the Atlantic and Gulf Coasts—to a 278-foot vessel used for worldwide oceanographic research and charting.

The administration maintains about a dozen different types of ships, each with specific design characteristics to suit her region of operation: the coasts of Alaska and the Pacific Northwest; the Atlantic Coast south to the Gulf of Mexico; and the Caribbean. Some appear to be fishing vessels, other deep-sea tugs, and, since all are painted white, the larger resemble Coast Guard cutters. The predominant identifying feature is the black-outlined hull number over the bold "NOAA" markings on the bows. The number is preceded by an **R** or an **S,** indicating **research** or **survey.** The R vessels principally conduct fisheries and living marine resources research, whereas the **S** vessels are engaged in hydrographic surveys and nautical charting.

When there's a stack it may be marked with three bands, one black and two blue, each of a different shade. You may also find a round logo of blue and black separated by the wings of a white seagull.

OCEAN SURVEILLANCE SHIP, NOAA

Designed to tow sonar gear to detect enemy submarines, ocean surveillance ships have in recent years been employed less and less in their intended mission. Some have been transferred to other government agencies. Two, still painted gray, are now carrying NOAA markings on their stacks, and are engaged in oceanographic survey and research work.

FISHING FOR A LIVING

For most seamen, being at sea is a two-dimensional experience: The world is laid out like a game board with grids and numbers; the seaman's job is to get his boat across the chart as quickly and safely as possible. The fisherman must add to this an elusive and shifting phantom beneath the surface. Where are the fish? Sonar can confirm their presence, but the skipper has to find them first.

These guys are out there all the time, in beautiful sunrises as well as morning skies filled with rain and sleet. Sometimes the ocean is flat and glassy, dotted with floats gone adrift from Japanese fishing nets thousands of miles away; other days, each onrushing sea threatens to wash the length of the boat.

Commercial fishermen seldom write adventurous sea stories for boating magazines extolling their seamanship; their record speaks for itself. Given the numbers of boats at sea, the losses are small. Fishermen have always had a healthy respect for the weather and are quick to stay in harbor if the reports are ominous.

If the fisherman has one weakness that will override his better judgment concerning wind and sea, it's his reluctance to stop bringing aboard fish. The hold can be full, but should there still be legal-sized fish in the net or on the line, and the boat isn't violating any laws except those of physics, he'll try, somehow, to get them aboard.

The skipper with his crew will load down the boat until the sea laps the weather deck. Nine hundred ninety-nine times out of a thousand he'll get her back to port; if he runs into sleet and snow when overloaded, though, he has a problem. A few tons of ice added topside to an overloaded boat in a nasty sea have been the end of more than one boat and crew.

SHRIMP TRAWLER, SOUTHEAST UNITED STATES

The typical southern shrimp trawler is a wooden vessel of limited length, originally rigged only for shrimping, which lacks the power and cruising range to compete in other markets. They're adaptable enough to handle flounder nets, but do not have the power to pull scallop dredges. Most are individually owned (as in the movie *Forrest Gump*) rather than part of a corporate fleet, so their profit margins are small. Proper maintenance and the luxury of a full crew are often sacrificed to reduce costs.

The southern shrimper is generally painted white, trimmed in black, and streaked with rust. Most are quite battered where the "doors" of the nets are brought alongside before being hauled aboard. Frequently a propane gas tank, used to fuel the galley stove, is visible on the outside of the deckhouse.

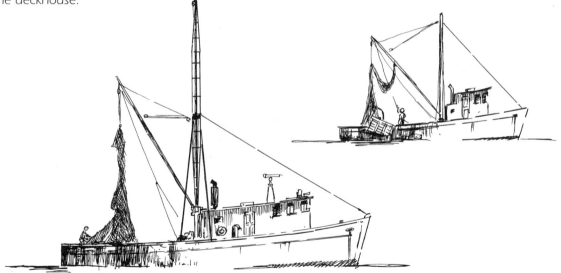

WHAT SHIP IS THAT?

EAST COAST TRAWLER

The steel-hull trawler used along the Atlantic Coast and the Gulf of Mexico is in reality a combination fishing vessel, capable of sailing to and engaging in the most profitable market available at the time; with little more than the shifting of some cables and blocks, the boat can pull midwater nets for shrimp, bottom nets for flounder, or a bottom dredge for scallops. These boats and their (typically) seven-man crew usually spend about two weeks on the fishing grounds.

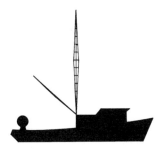

With changing fishing techniques, the large outriggers on these trawlers are being used less often for their intended purpose of towing extra nets; they're now sometimes lowered outboard to tow a suspended weight. This assembly produces a "dampening" effect on the boat's rolling motion in heavy seas.

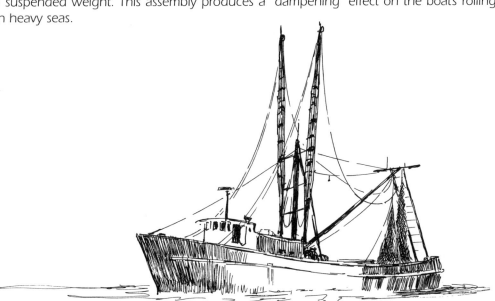

YOU'D BETTER WATCH OUT FOR YOUR
FINGERS AND TOES!

WHAT SHIP IS THAT?

MENHADEN PURSE SEINER

The menhaden seiner is easy to identify by the pilothouse forward, a tall mast with an observation platform, a long, low fish well amidships, and another deckhouse and stack aft. The positive stamp of identity? Two aluminum purse boats in davits at the stern.

The procedure for harvesting menhaden starts in the late afternoon, when the pilot of a light fixed-wing aircraft spiraling overhead scouts a section of the coast for signs of a promising school of fish. Factoring in the known migratory habits of the menhaden, ocean currents, and existing weather, the pilot advises the menhaden vessel's skipper of the anticipated location of the school for the following day; aircraft and seiner will rendezvous there early the next morning.

The trick is to launch the two purse boats and their crews, each with half of the net, and surround as much of the school of menhaden as possible before the fish go deeper into the sea. Directed by the pilot, the two 30- to 40-foot purse boats circle the school of fish, paying out the 1,200-foot net until they meet and join the ends. A line rove along the foot of the net is then hauled aboard the purse boats until the "purse" is closed at the bottom, preventing the fish from escaping.

The net is taken back aboard the two boats until the fish are concentrated in a confined pocket called the **bunt.** The mother ship comes alongside, lowers a 10-inch flexible hose, and pumps the fish into the tank amidships, where they're held until making their final voyage to the company processing plant, to be rendered into oil and fish meal. Unlike other commercial fish, the menhaden have already been contracted to buyers at an agreed-upon price.

Modern-day menhaden fishing bears some similarity to nineteenth-century whaling: The business of locating menhaden, launching boats, and chasing occurs independently of the mother ship. As in whaling, wages are based upon the quantity of fish taken, and one of the end products is oil. The menhaden fisherman no longer uses a man at the masthead to direct the operation, but then a Nantucket whaling skipper would've used an airplane if one had been available.

SCALLOP DRAGGER, EASTERN RIG

There have been few modifications to the fishing gear on this boat since she was first built many years ago—no outriggers added, no net reels installed on her stern. She has only her original mast and boom, positioned well forward, for handling nets or a dredge over the sides. This is the way, until recently, it was always done.

Among things nautical, commercial fishing is the saltiest of all. Fishing runs a tight race with sail in the salty sweepstakes, but the skipper of a sailing vessel, with a few exceptions, can choose his weather, or call it quits in the middle of a race. Only egos are damaged when a sailing voyage is aborted or a race is lost; the crews and owners seldom suffer real economic setbacks.

Although most sailboat people can reduce a sun sight for a fix or splice an eye in a line, few fishing skippers and maybe not one in a thousand crew members can do these seamanly things. Challenge him over his lack of mastery of nautical basics and the fisherman will inquire how much more money he could earn by calculating current vectors or time-speed-distance problems. After all, he has a piece of electronic gear that can provide the same information faster, more easily, and with greater accuracy. He's out there to catch fish, deliver them to the dock, and collect money— a serious business in which much is invested.

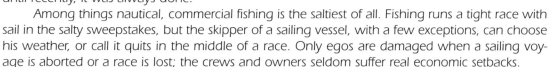

In New England, **Eastern** means east of Cape Cod; **Western** means west of Cape Cod. Eastern-rig boats haul nets and dredges over the side, lying broad-on to the wind. This can be uncomfortable in sloppy seas, and the crew is continuously exposed to the elements. Western-rig boats, which now dominate the industry nationwide, can jog head-on to heavy seas, their crews protected by the pilothouse. But old mariners say that there's never been a better sea boat than an Eastern-rig dragger; her low aft superstructure forms a natural weather vane that keeps the bow headed just off the wind should she lose power. And to many eyes, an Eastern-rig boat is far and away the better looker of the two. But she can't handle nets as fast or as efficiently, and is quickly disappearing from the scene.

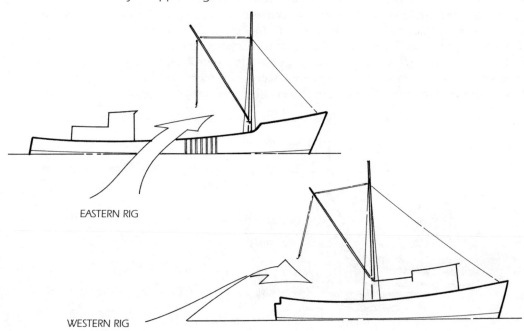

EASTERN RIG

WESTERN RIG

WEST COAST HALIBUT SCHOONER

The West Coast halibut schooners still fishing today were built in the 1920s and '30s, the direct descendants of a number of vessel types, both sail and steam, used in the halibut fishery since 1888. A pleasing sheer and the retention of the two-mast design from the old sailing fleet lend continuity with her heritage. With a seaworthy hull perfectly suited for the trade, the halibut schooner has survived replacement by more modern boats by continuously upgrading her fishing gear, power plant, and navigational and communications systems. Technological advances in hydraulically operated deck equipment and the installation of refrigeration have reduced the stiff labor requirements of her early years to a level that makes the halibut schooner competitive with new boats. The halibut schooner gets high praise: She's a proper boat.

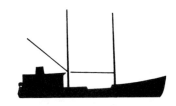

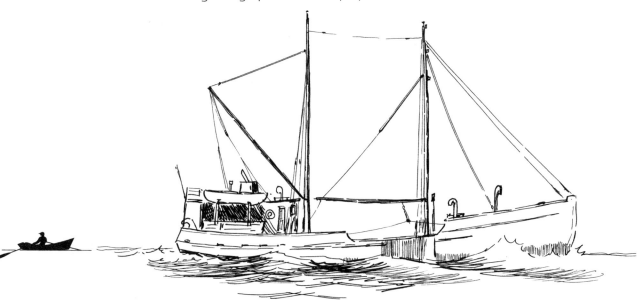

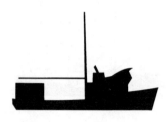

LONGLINER

After 1930, new boats built for the halibut fleet were also rigged for other fisheries, and by 1940 boats previously engaged as trollers and gillnetters were re-rigged and outfitted to extend their fishing ability to longlining for halibut. With all of these boats performing so many tasks, it's difficult to identify a specific design as a longliner. A number of longliners also fish in New England, primarily for groundfish like cod and haddock. Longliners are particularly popular in Atlantic Canada.

A predominant feature of a boat engaged in longline fishing is the baiting shed constructed on the stern. Used to protect crew members while they're baiting hooks and paying out the groundline, the baiting shed is a boxlike fabrication of an aluminum-tubing or light-wood framework, covered with colorful polyethylene tarpaulins or thin plywood. The structure is a simple and economical "add-on" for boats converting from other fisheries. Longliners are recognizable by the clusters of orange buoys hanging over their sides or lining the decks. Look for racks of floating flagpoles in the vicinity of the baiting shed.

The groundline comes in 1,800-foot lengths called **skates.** The baited hooks are attached to four- to five-foot-long branch lines, called **gangions,** spaced along the groundline at regular intervals. Today, most gangion lines are spaced at 18, 21, or 26 feet. The spacing is determined by the ability of the boat to retrieve, remove the fish, bait, and coil the lines. The total length of a longline may be as many as twelve skates (four miles). The length depends upon a number of factors, including sea conditions, the configuration of the bottom, and the suspected number of available fish.

The groundline is anchored at both ends and marked with a buoy and flag—or sometimes with a light—and left to "soak" for twelve hours. If it remains on the bottom for more than forty-eight hours, the bait, and the halibut, may fall prey to other sea-roving predators or scavengers.

FREEZER/LONGLINER

The gulf between the first sailing vessels taking halibut off the coast of Washington State and the diesel-powered halibut schooner is not very wide. The boats grew in size, steam replaced sail, and diesel replaced steam, but the intervals of change were long and the changes incremental. By comparison, the modern freezer/longliner is a major leap forward. The one shown here is 135 feet long, has a crew of twenty-four, and has a fish hold with a capacity of 666,000 pounds.

PACIFIC TUNA CLIPPER

If not for her large-diameter, towerlike mast and hefty boom, the tuna clipper could easily be mistaken for a luxury yacht. The clipper is fast and stylish, and the owners don't skimp on funds for appearance and maintenance.

Fishing-boat designers seem to be the last naval architects who'll draw a pleasant sheer for a hull. They must have some people around who still work with splines and ducks on the drawing board, rather than producing a set of lines and offsets with computers. Maybe there's something more personal about designing a fishing vessel. Maybe the designer can relate to the life of the fisherman more than that of a forklift operator on an 800-foot RO/RO. Then again, maybe fishermen just demand good-looking vessels.

Note the stack: It's off-center to starboard, to allow unobstructed deck space when the catch is being boarded over the port side.

ALASKAN PURSE SEINER

Also called a "58-foot-limit boat," referring to a conservation law that limits the size of boats in the fishery, the purse seiner catches fish moving in large schools (primarily salmon and herring) by encircling them with a long net equipped with floats on the top line and weights on the lower. After bringing the two ends of the net together, a line reeved along the bottom edge of the net is drawn taut, forming a bowl shape that prevents the fish from escaping by going deep. Purse seiners may also be rigged for shrimp or flounder trawling.

CATCHER/TRAWLER/PROCESSOR

Designed to operate in the North Pacific and the Bering Sea in search of crabs and flounder, the catcher/trawler/processor has the space and personnel aboard to process and freeze her own catch—a kind of floating frozen-fish factory that can stay at sea for extended periods.

NORTH PACIFIC CRAB BOAT

108' CRAB BOAT

Today's fisherman doesn't look like a character from *Captains Courageous* or the chap on the sardine can. He's more likely to sport a baseball cap emblazoned with JON DEERE or PENNZOIL than wear a sou'wester and an oiled-wool turtleneck sweater. Commercial fishing is listed as one of the most dangerous occupations in the country. There are few, if any, protective guards around deck machinery, and the sea is always trying to come aboard and wash his feet out from under him. Everything is wet and slippery, steel cables and booms are clanging about, and the sudden lurch of the boat will tip him over the side in a moment. Falling overboard is not something that happens in slow motion. One minute you're on deck, and the next you're in the water. The honky-tonk cowboy, so good at staying on the mechanical bull, would find a rolling and pitching Alaskan crab boat more than he could handle. Fall off here and it may be all over for you.

The North Pacific crab boat can be identified by the forward location of the house and mast, and the long boom for handling the crab pots. Of course, sighting a vessel on her way in or out with a deckload of wire pots makes for a positive identification.

COMBINATION CRABBER/TRAWLER

The North Pacific crab boat is a versatile vessel. This one is still more crab boat than trawler, but with her added trawling gear and net reel she can extend the season by trawling for shrimp and flounder.

This trawler/crabber has had her long boom replaced by a hydraulic crane, which makes handling gear considerably easier.

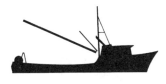

108' CRAB BOAT WITH NET REEL

TRAWLER CRABBER

GILLNETTER

West Coast gillnetters generally are about 30 to 40 feet long, and can be identified by the roller on the transom and the large drum for retrieving and stowing the net. Gillnets, as their name implies, catch fish by entangling their gills in the mesh. Some control over the size of fish harvested can be obtained by sizing the mesh to allow larger or smaller fish to pass through. In the Pacific, gillnetters most often target salmon. On the East Coast, gillnetters go after bottom fish such as cod and haddock.

CHESAPEAKE BAY OYSTERMAN

The man is more the story here than the boat. Standing on a narrow, wet washboard with no harness or life jacket, working a pair of oyster tongs (two rakes on long poles joined like a pair of scissors), the oysterman works all of a winter's day to bring up a few bushels of oysters, with no control over the price they'll bring at the agent's dock.

The average oyster boat—which is also used for crab potting—is built of wood; about 30 feet long; most able and seaworthy; open to the weather (with the exception of a trunk cabin forward); gasoline- or diesel-powered; and named after a female member of the owner's family.

Suspicious of everyone who lives more than a mile from his creek, a skepticism and mistrust inherited from his seventeenth-century waterman ancestors, today's oysterman is especially weary of tourists, biologists, ecologists, water resources commissions, and government inspectors of boats and oysters. Convinced that oysters are his, his grandfather's, his father's, and his son's by divine right, he wishes only to be left alone to harvest them.

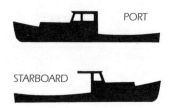

PORT

STARBOARD

JONESPORT LOBSTERBOAT

Fishing day in and day out in some of the harshest weather on the East Coast, the Maine-style lobsterboat is a perfect combination of aesthetics and efficiency. Light, fast, fuel-stingy, and supremely seaworthy, these craft evolved from Canadian fishing boats brought to the little towns of Jonesport and Beals Island, Maine, hence their familiar name—Jonesporters. The originals were built of cedar planks on oak frames. These days, fiberglass has largely replaced wood. Jonesporters are known for their speed. The typical 32-footer will do 25 mph with a 170-horsepower diesel or a converted automobile engine. At the popular lobsterboat races held up and down the Coast of Maine, boats running in the modified class, using dragster-style V-8s equipped with hot cams and other go-fasts, may run upward of 50 mph. These are workboats! Speed is important in the industry. The typical lobsterman handles between 400 and 1,000 traps a day, and the catch must be delivered alive.

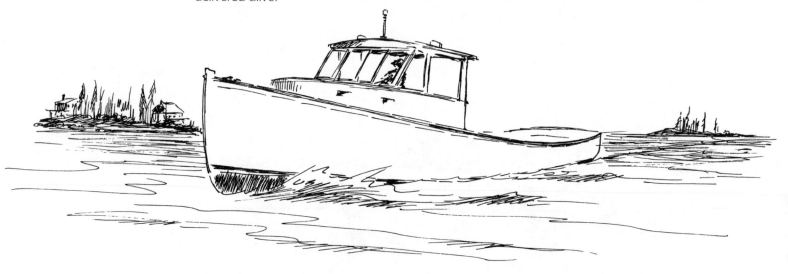

UNDER SAIL

The sailing vessels here are the ones you're most likely to encounter in ports around the world today. That's not to say that I can include in this slim volume all the various combinations of square and fore-and-aft sails out there. The presentation of square-rigged vessels is simplified for quick reference. To establish vessel types, I'm using only the silhouettes and profiles presented by the sails. You're unlikely to see one of these vessels under sail except at sea, and even if the vessel is under sail she may be shortened down and not carrying all her canvas—making the silhouettes here confusing at best. If there's no square sail set, you'll have to look for the presence and locations of yards on the masts.

A positive classification of rig is determined by the design of the spars (masts, boom, yards, bowsprits, gaffs), the details of which are less visible to the observer than are the sails. Unfortunately, technicalities governing the placement of masts and yards are often confusing and seemingly contradictory, especially to a novice trying to sort out the difference between a brigantine and a topsail schooner.

I can give you one absolute, though: There's no such rig as a "tall ship." The term comes from the poet John Masefield's yearnings for ". . . a tall ship, and a star to steer her by."

BARK, FOUR-MAST

The bark is a vessel with three or more masts, setting square sails on all masts except the aftermost, which is rigged with fore-and-aft sails. A fine example of an active four-mast bark is the Russian training vessel *Kruzenshtern*. German-built, 375 feet long, and setting 4,350 square yards of canvas, she can reach speeds of 16 to 17 mph in a proper breeze. Unlike so many training vessels, she is very well proportioned.

The quickest way to introduce young boys and girls to the physics of wind and water, and the influence of these natural forces upon a boat hull, is to start them with their own 8-foot sailing pram. One sail, a rudder, a daggerboard, a paddle, and a life jacket should be enough to fit her out. After one summer with the yacht club junior fleet, or just mucking about in some backwater creek, the kids will forever know more about handling big boats, or even ships, than the children given deep-vee runabouts with 75-horsepower outboards, trimmed out with control consoles, windshields, Bimini tops, bucket seats, depth finders, and gimbal mounts for soft-drink cans.

Most maritime nations maintain a sail-training vessel for naval and merchant cadets for just this reason. Prior to World War II, some European governments required young officers to serve time in commercial sailing ships before receiving a master's certificate for steamships. The result was a surplus of aspiring cadets eager for berths in a rapidly shrinking commercial sailing fleet—men willing to crew for no wages, who often paid their own upkeep for the privilege of sailing as seamen on the last of the working square-riggers. The most famous of these vessels employing free labor worked in the nitrate and wool trade, sailing from the west coast of South America and from Australia to England and Germany. A seaman who'd sailed from Sydney to the Horn and up the Atlantic to the Channel on a four-mast bark—loaded deep until the sea was only six to eight feet from the weather deck, working heavy canvas, wire ropes, chains, and steel yards—was simply cut from better cloth than the seaman who had not.

You can capture at least a little of the exhilaration of sailing a great bark by going aboard the *Peking,* permanently moored at South Street Seaport in New York City. Stand at her wheel. Wipe out the skyline of the city, imagine her decks awash, her sail shortened down to lower topsails, and the wind screaming so loud you can't hear a man next to you shouting.

RUSSIAN TRAINING BARK AT
THE CUSTOMHOUSE IN
NORFOLK, VA

WHAT SHIP IS THAT?

BARK, THREE-MAST

A sailor has to force a windjammer to go where he wants her to go—not where she wants—using determination and physical strength. Any sailing vessel, from pram to bark, does indeed seem to have a mind of her own—more like a headstrong horse than an obedient power vessel. After a year or so under sail, a cadet develops skills useful throughout a career at sea, whether as a tug captain or in command of a great passenger liner.

You may only see training vessels in some centennial parade, bedecked with colorful signal flags (spelling nothing), as if pageantry were their only reason for existing. Not so! These training vessels may look like the decorative ships in calendar paintings or labels on bottles of Scotch, but they are serious machines indeed.

The commercial square-rigged vessel couldn't sail to windward anywhere near as well as a vessel rigged with fore-and-aft sails. Square-riggers were designed to follow the predictable and ever-present tradewinds, and their sailing orders were issued by the home office with instructions to follow established routes about the globe. The owners of the great steel wind-ships of the early twentieth century also required their skippers to keep detailed records of wind, weather, and current observations on their voyages. The reported data was compiled and analyzed by those who, only a few years later, would be called statisticians and bean counters. Time has always been money.

The advantage of square sails when running before the trade winds is apparent. The division of sails into small, manageable units facilitates selecting the proper amount of sail needed in any given wind strength to balance the driving forces against the hull's continuously changing pivot point.

The U.S. Coast Guard *Eagle* is perhaps the best known three-masted bark in this country.

A BARK SHORTENED DOWN FOR HEAVY
WEATHER, CARRYING ONLY TOPSAILS,
SPANKER, AND INNER AND OUTER JIBS

A BARK UNDER FULL SAIL. FROM BOW TO STERN: THE FOREMAST, MAINMAST, AND MIZZENMAST. THE SQUARE SAILS FROM HULL UP: THE COURSE, THE LOWER TOPSAIL, UPPER TOPSAIL, TOPGALLANT, AND ROYAL. THE FORE-AND-AFT SAILS FROM THE FOREMAST TO THE END OF THE BOWSPRIT: THE FORE-TOPMAST STAY-SAIL, INNER JIB, OUTER JIB, AND FLYING JIB. THE FORE-AND-AFT SAILS ON THE MIZZEN MAST: THE SPANKER AND THE GAFF TOPSAIL.

WHAT SHIP IS THAT?

BARKENTINE

A barkentine must have at least three masts, the foremast rigged only with square sails, the remainder with fore-and-aft sails. This definition pretty much says it all. Unfortunately, the rules for classification of rigs and boat types seem to have as many modifiers, disclaimers, and exceptions as the tax code. The Chilean training vessel *Esmeralda* would appear to be a four-mast barkentine, but you may find her in ship lists as a topsail schooner—even though she carries no fore-and-aft sails on her foremast. Take your pick. I prefer barkentine.

A visitor boarding a large square-rigged vessel is often surprised by the sheer massiveness of the rigging and sail-handling gear: ponderous blocks secured to galvanized deck fittings, steel masts four feet in diameter, unbelievably heavy canvas sails bent to steel yards controlled by wire rope and chain running gear. He soon becomes aware that he's been misled by calendar paintings of tea clippers gliding serenely under cloudlike spreads of fluffy canvas while old salts sit around on coils of line carving pictures into whalebone and smoking little clay pipes. A stroll around the decks of one of today's training ships will quickly dispel that bit of nostalgia. If you don't jump swiftly, you could lose fingers and toes on these things!

WHAT SHIP IS THAT?

SHIP

Today the term **ship** applies to all large seagoing vessels, but in the days of sail it meant only one thing: a sailing vessel with three or more masts, square-rigged on all of them.

I remember an old movie in which dour and puritanical social workers were trying to remove a young girl from the guardianship of a salty old lightkeeper. Trying to determine the state of her education, they handed the girl a drawing containing numerous objects, of which four were sailing vessels. When asked how many ships were on the page, she said, "None! There are only two barks, a brigantine, and a schooner."

Needless to say, such knowledge was held in little regard by the social workers. To them, they were all ships.

BRIG

The brig is a two-mast vessel carrying square sails on both the foremast and the mainmast. There is a fore-and-aft sail on the main, called the **spanker,** but this gaff sail does not compromise the requirements that a brig be fully rigged with square sails on both masts.

Some consider sail training vessels only nautical classrooms providing "atmosphere" for math classes conducted on an open deck—sort of a field trip with an emphasis on knot-tying and suntans. True, academies don't go about casually placing their cadets in harm's way, but the sea and weather make no distinctions between training and working vessels, and nature does not make allowances for newcomers or old-timers. As recently as June of 1995, the Spanish training brig *Maria Assumpta* went aground off the Cornish coast, sank, and broke up. It was all real enough for those lads.

BRIGANTINE

Rigged with square sails only on her foremast, and fore-and-aft rigged on her mainmast, a brigantine is confusingly similar to a two-mast topsail schooner. The brigantine is an attempt at compromise: She's faster downwind than a vessel with only fore-and-aft sails, but won't sail as close to the wind. She requires fewer crew members than a vessel rigged with square sails on both masts.

TOPSAIL SCHOONER

The topsail schooner has two or more masts, of the same height or increasing in height as they move aft, and all rigged with fore-and-aft sails. It's the square sails set on the fore topmast that make her a topsail schooner—*not* the triangular fore-and-aft topsails set over the gaff sails. The advantage of such a rig is that the square topsails provide additional driving power when the wind is favorable; when working close to the wind and maneuvering in tight areas, the crew can douse them completely and use only the fore-and-aft sails.

These days, a lot of schooners are engaged in the vacation trade. Most have good food and drink, and water toys available for the more active. If it's a snug nook with a book and blanket you want—you got it. But rest assured, most of these schooners are "real" boats, generally rigged as heavily as their working ancestors and quite able to sail for weeks offshore.

I was a guest aboard the Swedish three-mast topsail schooner *Mary Ellen* a few years back, when I'd already reached a respectable age. I informed the skipper that I wished to be included in the crew, and not with my fellow guests. Always glad to have an extra man aloft, he agreed readily.

As we got underway, I scrambled up the foremast and out onto a great, varnished wooden yard as quickly as the paid hands. The language barrier was no problem; I knew what had to be done, and all the rigging was where I expected it to be. Feet firmly planted in the foot ropes, stomach resting on the sail, upper body tilted forward, I removed the stops from the furled canvas and shoved the bulk of it off the yard. The crew on deck hauled it out smartly. No problem.

Off the yard, up the mast to the next yard, shake out the sail, wife on deck showing just the right mixture of pride and fear. Exhilarating! Back on deck, I rushed aft to help the deck crew with the huge gaff mizzen—a bit of a problem. Finally, two Swedes and I were assigned to haul up the main—a *real* problem. By now my wife was showing alarm for the state of my health, rationalizing that if this is the way he wants it, we'll just bury him at sea. This was not small-boat racing. Out of breath and blinded with sweat, I politely and tactfully disengaged myself from my new associates and went below to find my old pals in the air-conditioned saloon, all crisp and dry with gin and tonics—none short of breath, and not a rope-burned hand to be seen. The skipper was telling amazing sea stories, and the steward brought seafood hors d'oeuvres and flaky little pastries. It was going to be a fine day.

SCHOONER, FORE-and-AFT RIG

When you encounter the term **schooner** in books or movies, this is the ship they're talking about. In the early years of this century it was the rig of the Grand Banks fishermen, the coastal lumber trade, and grand yachts. The term is also misused by many writers, however, who'll call anything carrying sail a schooner.

SCHOONER WITH MAIN TOPSAIL

But there's no fog clouding the definition of a schooner: She has to have two or more masts of the same height or increasing in height as they move aft, and she must carry only fore-and-aft rigged sails. There are gaff schooners, staysail schooners, Bermuda-rigged schooners, and combinations of all of these; however, it's the masts that establish identity. She may carry topsails, but they have to be fore-and-aft-rigged triangular topsails; if she has square sails set on yards, she's a topsail schooner. The schooner may or may not have a bowsprit; either way, she's a schooner.

The schooner rig is most suitable for sailing perpendicular to the wind **(reaching)** or sailing in the same direction as the wind **(running);** she's not so good when sailing diagonally into the wind **(beating and tacking),** but she's still better at going to windward than is a square-rigged vessel. These features made schooners well suited for the American coasting trade. The skipper could choose the most favorable winds for long passages, but still had the ability to enter harbors if, upon arrival, he found the winds against him. The gaff-rigged sails of the classic schooner produce a driving force with a low center of effort, allowing them to be carried longer in high winds than tall rigs—a feature that provides comfort for the crew and seakeeping ability for the vessel.

It was snowing the morning I joined a 95-foot gaff-rigged schooner at the public dock in Annapolis. She was to sail for Norfolk at noon. My only credential for this enviable berth was the assurance to the captain from a friend of mine that I knew the ropes.

By midnight, the wind had backed into the northwest and the sky had cleared. We were broad-reaching down Chesapeake Bay with winds gusting to 50 mph, the bow spray sparkling red and green from the reflections of the running lights. I'd come up from a forward hatch, cautiously worked my way aft, identified myself to the man at the wheel, and received his instructions to hold her a tad west of 180. It was impossible to hear him; he indicated the course by putting his finger on the compass, and quickly disappeared. The previous watch had taken in all sail except a double-reefed foresail, and they'd all gone below. For the next two hours she was all mine. One of life's grand rewards.

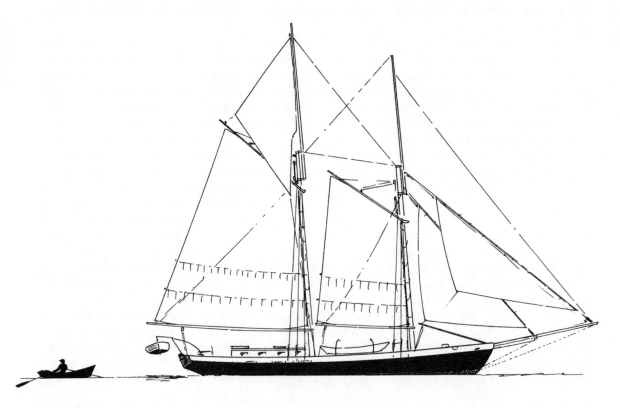

WHAT SHIP IS THAT?

SCHOONER, THREE-MAST

Three-mast schooners encountered in harbors and bays today are often engaged in day-trips, carrying paying customers on vacation. The three-masters are less common than their two-masted sisters. *The Victory Chimes,* a three-mast Chesapeake Bay "ram" now in the tourist business, was until the mid-1940s employed in the lumber trade under her original name, *Edwin and Maud.*

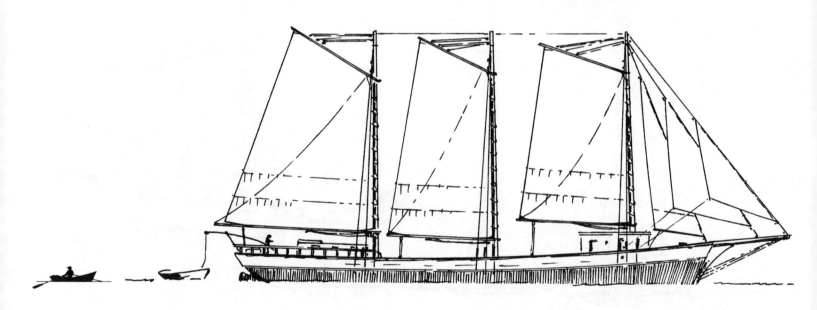

WHAT SHIP IS THAT?

KETCHES and YAWLS

No gray area here. On both ketches and yawls, the mizzenmast (the aftermost mast) is shorter than the mainmast. If both masts are the same height, or if the aftermost mast is taller, she's a schooner. But how do you tell the difference between a ketch and a yawl? On a ketch, the mizzenmast is located *forward* of the rudder post; on a yawl, the mizzen is *aft* of the rudder post. Trouble is, the determining technical factor is underwater. But you can get a fair indication of the rudder post's location by finding the tiller or the helm.

Where's the helmsman standing? Is he between the masts or aft of both of them? If he's between the masts you have a yawl; if aft of both masts, a ketch. Of course, some ketch owners may place a remote steering station far from where it should be, thus mucking up all of my guidelines. A yawl's mizzensail is considerably smaller than the mizzensail of a ketch, and the mast is located closer to the stern. I've heard the yawl rig described as a "catboat chasing a sloop."

KETCH

On a ketch, the mizzenmast is shorter than the mainmast and stepped *forward* of the rudder. Dropping the mainsail on a ketch will quickly reduce the sail area and will leave the boat reasonably balanced under the large mizzen and jib. This is a feature you'll most appreciate in a sudden squall, or if an urge arises to go below to make tea in a more upright and dignified position.

WHAT SHIP IS THAT?

YAWL

On a yawl, the mizzenmast is shorter than the mainmast and stepped *aft* of the rudder. Both ketch and yawl rigs provide a number of convenient combinations of sails adjustable to weather conditions. An anchored yawl with only its mizzensail set and sheeted-in tight will behave like a weather vane, remaining comfortably pointed into the wind.

WHAT SHIP IS THAT?

SLOOP

The rig of choice among most sailboat owners at present is the sloop. For the wealthy at the turn of the century it was the schooner; by the 1950s, the ketch was the boat most recommended for seakeeping abilities and comfort while cruising. No doubt the popularity of any particular rig is generated by the economy, technology, and fads of the time. Currently, the rules governing the design, building, and racing of sailing yachts favor the sloop. Among nonracing owners, the ease of handling a sloop (which requires only one or two crew members), and her cost relative to other rigs, has produced sloops as plentiful as herrings.

If the boat is anchored and has only one mast, call her a sloop. She could be a cutter or a catboat, but odds-on she's a sloop. If she's under sail, there will be a mainsail and one headsail, the jib. Should you observe two headsails and note that the mast is located almost in the middle of the boat, you may be looking at a cutter. I say "may be" because some argue that, even with two headsails, if the mast is closer to the bow than to the middle, the boat is still a sloop. A double-headsail sloop, to be precise.

When racing, either rig may carry a balloonlike spinnaker while running downwind; spinnakers don't count as headsails, so you can't use them to determine if you have a sloop or a cutter. Confusing? Call them all **sloops** and be done with it. If taken to task for your opinion, just say that the mast looks a bit too far forward for a cutter.

Sloops may have a gaff mainsail or a triangular mainsail (called a **Bermuda rig**). There may or may not be a bowsprit. Whatever. One mast, one mainsail, and one jib equals one sloop.

WHAT SHIP IS THAT?

GAFF-RIGGED SLOOP

You can sail a sloop singlehanded, but on a gaff-rigged boat it's nice to have an extra crewman or two along. That heavy gaff aloft can develop a mind of its own in a slop.

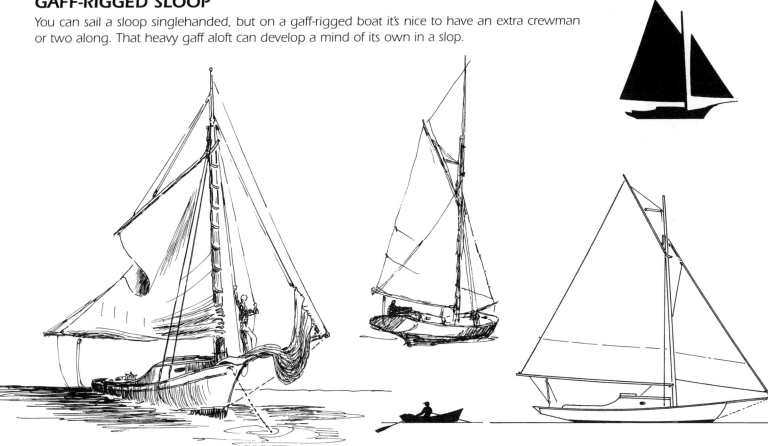

INTERNATIONAL 12-METER RACING-CLASS SLOOP

After a twenty-one-year period of America's Cup–racing inactivity, the New York Yacht Club declared the 12-meter class *the* boat to use to defend or challenge the "hundred guinea cup." Lacking the grandeur and magnificence of J-boats—last used in the cup races of 1937—the 12s were still sufficiently impressive in size and grace to a new generation of yacht-racing enthusiasts. They were also expensive enough to keep the number of challengers to a minimum.

"Twelve-meter" has nothing to do with the length of the boat. This is a dimensionless rating number mathematically arrived at after the boat has met fourteen pages of measurement requirements; she's then certified and pronounced a 12-meter. Actually, these boats are around 65 feet long.

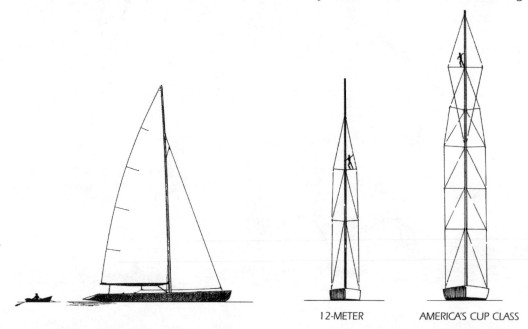

12-METER   AMERICA'S CUP CLASS

INTERNATIONAL AMERICA'S CUP–CLASS SLOOP

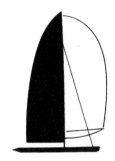

Replacing the 12-meter as the class designated to defend or challenge the America's Cup, the International America's Cup–Class is larger and faster than the 12-meter. Since it's a new class, we can expect impressive design breakthroughs in the coming years, and clever new ways to beat the new rules.

The availability of corporate money and the need for exciting television coverage of the America's Cup races have made the 12-meter unsuitable for the event. I suspect that the new boats, being much larger, provide a lot more space for advertising. When you consider that keels have fallen off, masts have snapped, and one boat has buckled in the middle and sunk into the Pacific, the America's Cup–Class is putting on a spectacular show.

In *Moby Dick*, when the *Pequod* sank, a masthead pennant ensnared a sky hawk and pulled it under with her—a symbolic moment, the meaning of which has been discussed in many an English literature class. When a cup boat sank off San Diego, one of the last symbols I saw was the mainsail logo of a famous manufacturer of sandwich spreads. This also may be discussed in future classrooms, but somehow it's just not the same.

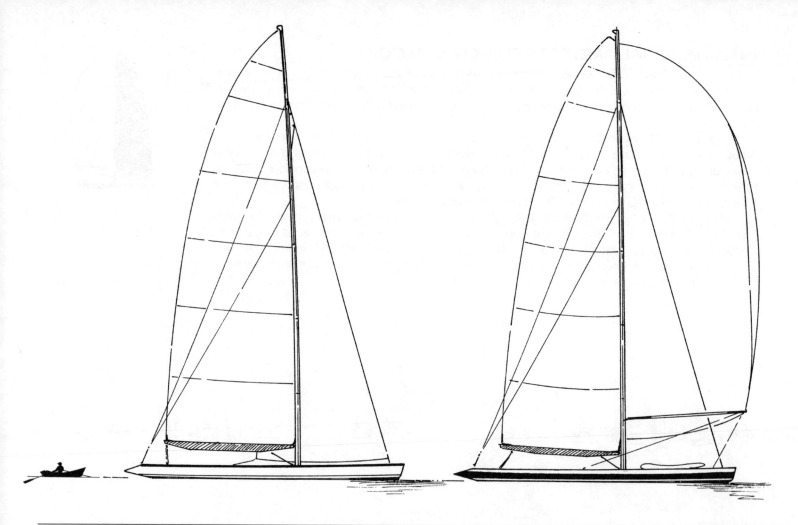

J-CLASS RACING YACHT

Only a couple of J-boats are around nowadays, but should you be lucky enough to see one, you will, in some small measure, link yourself with yachting history just by being in her presence. In the development of aircraft, trains, and ships, it seems as if grace, beauty, and harmony between machine and nature are eventually sacrificed to utility. That's a natural change; a vessel's purpose is to win races or make a profit. Still, there are those few years when technology and aesthetics are in sublime balance. In racing-yacht design, this moment surely came during the reign of the J-boats.

The *Ranger* and *Endeavor* II were the last Js to race for the America's Cup, in 1937. When the races were resumed in 1958, they were conducted with 12-meter sloops.

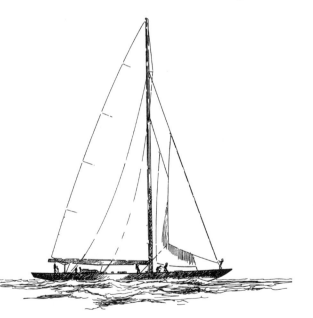

CUTTER

The cutter has one mast and three working sails: the mainsail, staysail, and jib. It's easy to mistake her for a sloop should the skipper be mucking along with only one headsail set. You'll have to consider the position of the mast for identification. Roughly, a sloop's mast is placed about one-third of the length of the boat from the bow. The mast of the cutter is closer to the middle of the boat.

You may ask, Why all this fuss about one headsail or two? The more sections you can divide the sail area into, the easier it is to handle. The more combinations of sails are available to suit varying wind or sea conditions, the safer it is to work on wet decks on dark nights. The disadvantages of the cutter's arrangement are the need for larger crews and some loss in the ability to sail to windward. Cutters are generally serious cruising boats, and often double-ended to present "two bows" to the sea.

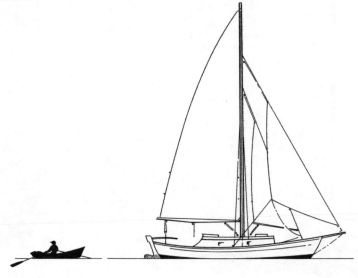

WHAT SHIP IS THAT?

CATBOAT

A number of small boats that have one mast carrying only one sail call themselves **catboats;** however, the name generally applies to the Cape Cod catboat, a classic workboat from the early 1900s, half as wide as she is long. The Cape Cod cat is trimmed out with a barn-door rudder hung on the transom; a mast with the heft of a telephone pole stepped inches from the bow stem; a boom projecting over the stern; and a gaff sail. There's nothing else like her. She's cranky and unforgiving, with far more reasons not to own one than otherwise. Still, catboat owners look with disdain upon other sailing craft, if they look at all. The difference between this rig and others is more than boat design. Here we get into philosophy.

SKIPJACK OYSTER SLOOP

To prevent overharvesting of oyster beds, the state of Maryland imposes restrictions on the use of engines for dredging oysters in state waters. As well as protecting the oyster, the restrictions have had the secondary effect of prolonging the life of the skipjack, the last working sailing vessel on the East Coast. With numbers down from as many as fifty in 1949 to less than a dozen in 1994, skipjacks account for only about four percent of the oyster harvest; the rest is taken with hand tongs. The remaining few skipjacks are working out of Maryland ports in the upper Chesapeake Bay.

Crewed by a skipper and two men to handle the sails and operate the gear, the skipjack pulls a dredge (basically a steel rake) from each side of the hull. Her pronounced low sides ease the task of hauling aboard the dredges. On special days, set aside by the regulations in specific oyster management programs, oystermen are allowed to use their push boats—sometimes called yawl boats—for the dredging operation. Installing an engine inside the skipjack itself is prohibited.

Difficulty in hiring crews, high boat-maintenance costs, aging boats, unpredictable market prices—all contribute to skipjacks' low profits relative to investment. Despite these harsh realities, artists and writers have romanticized the skipjack's role in the oyster trade, magnifying it far beyond its current importance. All the publicity has encouraged numerous institutions to propose ways to preserve the few remaining boats, from school ships to "working museums" for the enlightenment of city kids. If you want to see skipjacks engaged in honest work, however, you'd better go see them while you still can.

HEAD OF THE RIVER

7

I define *head of the river* as the place that begins where the harbor cruise boat turns around and starts back downtown. Tourists on a sight-seeing vessel, operating from a fashionable "harbor-view" shopping mall, are unlikely to be exposed to these sections of the river—embarrassments to the Harbor Beautification and Urban Waterfront Enhancement Committee.

Access to the companies and industries operating in the upper reaches of creeks and rivers is difficult. It's a world of chain-link fences and guard shacks that each contain a person with little sense of humor. There are interesting boats to be seen here, though, even if sometimes it takes a bit of deduction to establish what type of craft they are, or were. Recognizing old navy vessels, sold as surplus and converted for use in civilian jobs, is made difficult by altered housing and imaginative paint jobs.

About the only view visitors to the coast will have of such waters will occur if they're entering or leaving a port city via airplane, or circumventing the city on the beltway. Then, soon after takeoff or from a high-rise overpass, travelers may momentarily glimpse this less glamorous boating world. Briefly, they may appreciate the muted colors of rusty metal roofs and discarded shipping containers, and fleetingly observe the random patterns of shallow creeks, tidal flats, drainage ditches, and marsh grass. They may note the geometric rows and stacks of a thousand oil or paint drums, the files and columns of crippled earth-moving equipment, or the acres of wooden forklift pallets.

Here are abandoned piers whose creosoted pilings and decking catch fire with some regularity, and threaten nearby deposits of decaying canvas, cork, and kapok life jackets and life rings. Observers may wonder how 10,000 flotation devices of the *Titanic* variety ever came to one collective end.

At the head of the river are dozens of metal lifeboats, pumps, generators, winches, anchors, bent shafts, ventilation ducts, and pipes, all twisted and blended into one surrealistic sculpture. The scene may appear chaotic and without order, but all of its elements have been sorted according to worth. Mountains of aluminum scrap reflect the sun; mountains of steel scrap rust and bleed brown into patches of bare earth.

As the plane banks into a climbing turn and the headwaters give way to farms and woodlands, travelers, so recently on the sight-seeing boat, may realize that there was a lot of interesting stuff down there that they never got to check out.

THIS OLIVE OIL TANK
PROBABLY CONTAINS
UNTAXED DIESEL FUEL

Old, tired salvage ships, dropped from the navy lists, generally have a few more useful earning years left in them as large workboats for private shipyards and contractors. Already outfitted with everything you'd need for underwater exploring, a salvage ship of this class would be the proper vessel for treasure-hunting in warm waters. Should you find no silver plate or cannon or wine bottles, you can always rig the foredeck with a white awning and wicker chairs, and have some memorable late-evening conversations over rum drinks.

BREAKER'S YARD

It ends here, at the head of the river. The vessel has been "sold down" many times, and is no longer used for her intended purpose. She's come a long way from that summer day when the owner's daughter—fashionably trimmed out in white organza, with a pastel silk sash and bow and a big hat with ribbons and flowers like they wear at the Kentucky Derby—smacked the bow with a bottle of Dom Pérignon, and the new vessel slid off the builder's ways in a cloud of colored streamers and balloons. On that promising day, she had a rosy future; the owners were proud of their expertise in the market and their cleverness in investing so heavily. And probably rightly so. But markets change, steel rusts, and the vessel's cargo capacity will no longer pay for the cost of the fuel required to move her.

First she was sold to less demanding trades, and then to very dubious trades. Each time the vessel changed hands she was stripped of some piece of equipment that might bring in a little extra cash on the side. Going longer and longer between overhauls and paint jobs, the vessel changed colors like a chameleon until she blended into the very vegetation of the upper tributaries. The last time a "company" identified itself by painting its name on her rusty stern, the work seems to have been done with a five-inch brush by a chap who'd breakfasted on potted ham and gin.

After lying sunk up to her main deck for a year, she's now hauled ashore, foot by foot, and broken into salable scrap. Her flat plates, shapes, and angle bars are loaded onto battered railroad cars, also at the head of their own rusty trail.

Ships and boats flow in and out of the world's harbors, continuously renewing themselves, like plankton in and out of the marsh grass.

WHAT SHIP IS THAT?